HOLINESS
REVEALED

A DEVOTIONAL STUDY IN HEBREWS

AMY REARDON

wesleyan
PUBLISHING HOUSE
wphstore.com

CREST BOOKS

CONTENTS

Prologue   5

Introduction   8

Part 1. The Incomparable Christ (Heb. 1–2)   19

Part 2. The Perfect Rest (Heb. 3–5)   63

Part 3. The Real Promise (Heb. 6–8)   95

Part 4. The Better Covenant (IIeb. 9:1 — 10:18)   127

Part 5. The Practical Implications (IIeb. 10:19 — 11:31)   163

Part 6. The Final Outcome (Heb. 11:32 — 13:25)   195

Notes   230

For free study notes, visit our Shepherding Resources site:
www.wphresources.com/holinessrevealed.

PROLOGUE

The book of Hebrews is complex and full of tightly argued theology. As a literary work, it is masterful, but as a spiritual and theological guide, it can be quite challenging. However, many scholarly writings assist in wading through it. They give pages of detail and are truly fascinating. But this devotional study is meant to serve as a devotional with the aim of engaging both mind and heart.

This book is not for scholars, nor is it for beginners. It is for the Christian who is looking for a personal or group Bible study or devotion that involves both intellectual thought and inward reflection.

Some devotional books focus mostly on the personal application of Scripture. They include a rush to look within ourselves, to change, to fix, and simply to understand our own selves better. That is vital to be sure. But what is God revealing to us about who *he* is? The glorious Christology[1] of Hebrews addresses this question by bringing us face-to-face with the terrestrial expression of God: the God-man, Jesus Christ. And when God gives us a glimpse of who he is, we don't want to miss it.

Hebrews is not an easy read for the twenty-first-century Christian. One often stumbles and sometimes trips over its content. But the serious Bible student is not satisfied with just glossing over the tricky parts. A love for God and a love for his Word compel us to dig in, to try to really understand what is written. With some portions of Scripture, definitive interpretations are dangerous. Two readers can understand one passage completely differently, even if both readers are biblical scholars. Even so, if we really care about God's Word, we can't be afraid of it. We must approach it with alert minds and devoted hearts.

This book will not reveal all the mysteries of Hebrews. But it is my hope that it will aid in addressing the bulk of what Hebrews contains without sweeping chunks under the rug. Let's try to connect the dots of the themes running throughout the book. Let's try to tackle the parts that alarm us. And even when we can't figure it all out, let's try to make ourselves aware of what the difficulties are, instead of turning a blind eye to them. What do we stand to gain? As commentator Donald Guthrie has noted, the book of Hebrews will help us answer the most important question of all time—a question that incorporates both the idea of knowing God and knowing ourselves: How do human beings approach God?[2]

INTRODUCTION

Since the days of Adam and Eve, sin has always been with us. Even as I was in the process of writing this book, there was practically a reenactment of the garden of Eden in my own home. My young son had drawn a picture with a whiteboard marker on a small erasable board. I praised his picture and told him I wanted to show it to Daddy when he got home. My daughter, standing nearby, reached her finger toward the board to rub out the picture. As I snatched the picture before she could destroy it, she pouted and said, "I want to draw a picture, too."

"OK," I said. "Upstairs you have paper of all sorts. You have markers and crayons and colored pencils. You can draw anything you want! The only thing you can't do is draw on this one board."

"I want to draw on that board!" she hollered.

I couldn't help but think of our first parents. They wanted the one thing—*one thing* out of an entire garden—that they couldn't have. Of course, what they wanted wasn't so much a juicy piece of fruit as it was to be masters of their own fates. To be like God. To be in control. I'm pretty sure that's what my daughter wanted too.

As we all know, it was that egotistical sin that separated us from our holy God. Eventually, God formalized a covenant that would establish a means of human-divine relationship. He would be the God of the Israelites, and they would be his people. But they were expected to fulfill certain obligations—laws—in order to please God and connect with him. Above all, there had to be payment for sin. That took place in the form of animal sacrifice. But in God's good time, a new covenant was brought about because of the life and saving work of Jesus.

The book of Hebrews is written to prove that God's new covenant is an improvement upon the old system. That is not to say that God had made some sort of error with the first covenant. Rather, the original covenant was just a shadow of things to come. Hebrews 10:1 says, "The law is only a shadow of the good things that are coming—not the realities themselves. For this reason it can never, by the same sacrifices repeated endlessly year after year, make perfect those who draw near to worship."

Jesus brought complete, perfect salvation. His sacrifice was once and for all and provided us with access to the

Father. In addition, he sent us the Holy Spirit, enabling us to live completely sanctified lives. These are the "good things" God promised. The shadow has been lifted. We live in the full light of the work and glory of Christ. We can be made perfect in him.

In exploring the amazing thing God has done, the book of Hebrews falls into three major sections. The first section comprises the first three parts of this book and shows readers who Jesus really is. Hebrews indulges us with some of the Bible's loveliest, most poetic Christology. It is thorough, exploring Jesus and his work almost exclusively for seven entire chapters. The main point of the first section is to prove that Jesus is a superior mediator between God and man. (I must acknowledge that the biblical text does not actually use the word *mediator* until chapter 8, which is in the second section of the book. However, the word so perfectly sums up what is taught in the first section that I felt free to make use of it.)

The second section is found in part 4, and it explores the covenant. It discusses the temporal status the first covenant had and the perfection and permanency of the second. Its main point is to prove that the first covenant was incomplete, and the second has replaced it.

With the third section (parts 5 and 6), the writer becomes pastoral. In view of all Christ has done, our response should involve our constancy. We are to be loving in all our relationships and lead disciplined lives. In this section we also find the famous chapter on heroes of the faith, worthy examples of Christian commitment.

This book is divided into thirty-one devotional studies. It will also be helpful to have your Bible open to Hebrews and a notebook on hand as you read and reflect. The devotions in this book are not all equal in length, as some portions of the book of Hebrews are more complex than others. Questions follow each devotion, but some have fewer questions than others. The book has six parts that are each suited to a week's study for groups or individuals. You may wish to do one a day (five or six in a week), but if some Scripture portion really begins to dig into your soul, take your time.

Before we begin, however, it's important to take a look at the setting of the book: the author, the recipients, and the date of writing. Frankly, not much is known. But there are some educated guesses, and the text is better understood when the possibilities of the setting are considered.

May the Holy Spirit work in your life, speaking to both your intellect and your soul as you explore this rich portion of the Word of God.

THE SETTING OF HEBREWS

So much is unknown about Hebrews. While other Epistles have an identified author and audience, Hebrews leaves us guessing. Often, knowing the writer's or the recipients' situation makes a book come alive. For example, aren't we moved that Paul could write to the Philippians about rejoicing while he was chained in prison? Aren't we more inspired by the faithfulness of the Thessalonians, knowing they were suffering persecution?

Even without certainty of the details, Hebrews is a gold mine for Christians. Our hearts fill with gratitude when we realize what Christ has done for us. We jump at the chance to respond by imitating great saints of the past and give a ready ear to the admonishments toward the end of the text. Still, we can enrich our experience by considering theories about the background of the book.

WHO WROTE HEBREWS?

If you open a King James Bible, you'll see credit given to Paul as the author of the epistle. But you won't see that in *The New International Version* or in most other translations. Paul's name is not found in the oldest Greek manuscripts, and many of the church fathers—much closer in time to the writing of the book than King James' team—did not believe Paul wrote it. Donald Guthrie says that now, in the twenty-first century, "Pauline authorship is almost universally regarded as unacceptable."[1] But because for centuries Paul was believed to be the writer, it is worthwhile to review a few of the facts that persuaded scholars otherwise. Here are three reasons that Guthrie notes.

First, the author never gives a name. Paul always used his name in his letters. He had a personal relationship with most of the churches to which he wrote, having visited the majority of them, so including his name only made sense. In addition, Paul used his good name for its credibility. The message of the letter was nearly always readily accepted when his name appeared in it.[2]

Second, the writing of Hebrews doesn't sound like that of Paul. The Greek is too sophisticated for him, and the letter is quite focused. Paul's letters tend to have a bit of rabbit-trailing that is not found in Hebrews, and his style of Greek was a bit more commonplace.

Third, the subject matter doesn't resemble that of Paul's other letters. Paul demonstrated consistency as he wrote to different people and churches. But we don't find his favored themes in Hebrews. Also, much of what *is* in Hebrews isn't echoed in Paul's other letters. Gareth Cockerill gives an example: "[The author of Hebrews] is more interested in the kind of faith that enables a Christian to persevere in the face of difficulties (11:1–40) than in Paul's more frequent theme: the kind of faith through which one becomes a Christian (Rom. 1:16; 5:1–5; Eph. 2:8–9)."[3]

Scholars have suggested many possible authors, including Apollos, Philip, Peter, Jude, and even Priscilla. Some may be surprised to see a woman's name in this list. The people of that day would have been equally surprised! In fact, one of the reasons Priscilla is suspected is because no author's name is given. If a woman had written it, she might well have left her name off, since many people would have rejected a letter with female authorship. But why is this woman in particular considered as a possible author? She and her husband both served as theological instructors to Apollos, so she was an important teacher (Acts 18:24–26). Paul considered her his coworker, which underscores her status as a respected woman of the church (Rom. 16:3). Of the few prominent women with whom the New Testament acquaints us, she seems most likely.

It is exciting to think that a woman could have written a book of the Bible. But most likely, the authorship of Hebrews will remain a mystery until we meet the author face-to-face! One thing is certain: Hebrews is one of the most beautifully crafted Epistles in the New Testament. Peter O'Brien, who refers to the writer as a "creative theologian," offers the following praise: "His writing has been regarded by many as the finest in the New Testament, both in its use of grammar and vocabulary and in its style and knowledge of Greek rhetorical conventions. He was probably trained in rhetoric, as his use of alliteration, antithesis, chiasm, and many other stylistic elements attests, and he is familiar with philosophy, both Jewish and Greek."[4] Unfortunately, most of us read the epistle in English, not ancient Greek, so we lose much of the style and grace of the writing.

It is only fair to acknowledge that it would be rare for a woman to have been trained so extensively. (Why not a woman with extraordinary natural gifts, not to mention the inspiration of the Holy Spirit?) What really matters is that the book is the inspired Word of God, and as such it is "alive and active" (Heb. 4:12). If we recognize that God directed the process, the person who actually put words to papyrus is fairly inconsequential.

Because we have no name for the writer, we will often see him or her referred to as "the writer" or "the author." These terms do not refer to the writer of this devotional study, but to the person who penned Hebrews.

FOR WHOM WAS THE BOOK WRITTEN?

Although the book is called "Hebrews," it isn't quite clear for whom it was written. It might have been for Jewish Christians in Jerusalem. It might have been for Jewish

Christians elsewhere. Or, despite its nomenclature, it might have been written for Gentiles.

One can't read Hebrews without noticing all the Old Testament passages quoted and, of course, all the discussion about Jewish faith and practices. But the quotes are from the Septuagint, the Greek translation of the Hebrew Bible. This may indicate that the intended audience was non-Jewish. As converts to the Christian faith, the readers would have become familiar with the Septuagint quickly, since there was no canonized Christian Bible yet. In so doing, they may have been asking questions as to how all the business of priests and sacrifices related to them, which is a major subject of Hebrews.[5]

If the intended audience was actually Jewish, the recipients may have been living outside Palestine. The text mentions that none of them had actually heard Jesus himself. That would be a stretch if the community were in Jerusalem. The use of the Septuagint, rather than the Bible of the Hebrews (the *Tanakh*[6]), makes Jerusalem a remote choice. There is also a heavy Hellenistic (Greek) influence in the book, which is why places such as Alexandria are suggested. Many other cities have been proposed, one of which is Rome. Rome is often considered the strongest possibility.

We can be confident that the recipients of the letter were in an urban area of the Roman Empire, just as is true of the other epistles to church communities. The favored theory seems to be that the audience was a community of Jews somewhere other than Jerusalem. F. F. Bruce notes that the writer's great conviction about the old covenant being replaced by the new wouldn't have had much zing if it weren't written to people who were accustomed to following the Hebrew faith—that is, Jews.[7] And Cockerill notes that Greek-speaking Jews were very caught up in God revealing himself through Moses[8]—a subject the writer used to make his argument about the supremacy of Jesus.

As we try to understand Hebrews in the twenty-first century, it may not matter too much if the recipients lived in Rome, Jerusalem, or wherever. It helps to know, however, that this group of believers had suffered insult, imprisonment, and persecution—although none had been martyred (Heb. 10:32–35). They were beginning to back away from their faith, and it seems they wished to return to the traditional Hebrew ways. Perhaps that isn't too surprising when we consider that while persecution was beginning to heat up for Christians, the Jewish faith was still protected by Roman law. When we think of the challenges they faced and their temptation to turn tail and run back to something more familiar, we may be able to apply the lessons in Hebrews to our own personal situations in a more meaningful way.

WHEN WAS HEBREWS WRITTEN?

The date for the writing is hard to determine when we cannot verify the author and audience. However, we do have one enormous clue. The book of 1 Clement is dated at about AD 96. That book quotes Hebrews. So the book of Hebrews must have been written before AD 96.

A few other clues are key. Hebrews mentions Timothy, and it is believed that this is the same Timothy who accompanied Paul. So the book would have been written during Timothy's lifetime. The lack of mention of Paul may indicate that Paul was no longer alive. He died around AD 67.

Hebrews makes no mention of the destruction of the temple and the conquering of Jerusalem in AD 70. In fact, the book seems to be written to address the regular, continuing practice of temple activities that would have ceased in AD 70.[9] Writing a book like Hebrews without mentioning the destruction of the temple really doesn't make sense. This seems a strong indication that the book was written before the year AD 70.

PART 1

THE INCOMPARABLE
CHRIST

HEBREWS 1–2

WHO CHRIST IS, PART 1

HEBREWS 1:1–4

GOD'S COMMUNICATION BEFORE CHRIST
(HEB. 1:1)

The Lord had been communicating with his people for centuries before the incarnation of Jesus Christ. The Old Testament is full of stories of this communication. The writer of Hebrews mentioned prophets as deliverers of God's Word, and implied that angels did the same. The emphasis in Hebrews 1:1 is on the prophets.

The deeds of some of the prophets were sometimes so bizarre they might have qualified them as mentally unfit if they weren't known to be men of God. Think of Ezekiel lying on his left side for 390 days and for 40 days on his right, all the while eating only a starving man's rations prepared over cow dung (Ezek. 4). Think of Hosea purposefully marrying a prostitute (Hos. 1). These were not acts of insanity. These were powerful, living metaphors that communicated God's displeasure with Israel.

A prophet might do a spectacular thing, as when Elijah called down fire from heaven to ignite a sopping wet altar (1 Kings 18). He might see visions, as Isaiah (ch. 6) and Zechariah (chs. 1–6) did. Or a prophet might just preach or guide, as seems to have been the case with the prophets Micah and Nahum.

Enemies ran in fear of prophets, and kings submitted to them. If a person received the blessing of a prophet, it meant that person received the blessing of God. Although the prophets were often isolated from the rest of the population, their status in society was well established. They were God's human mouthpieces.

GOD'S NEXT COMMUNICATOR (HEB. 1:2–4)

Verse 2 opens with "in these last days." That was written millennia ago, yet we are still waiting for the return of Christ. How does the first century qualify as "last days"?

Jews and early Christians, similar to ourselves, viewed all of salvation history to be in two major eras. The first era is full of prophecy and prediction about the future. The second era is the fulfillment of the prophecies. The Greek term translated as "last days" is more accurately translated as "this final age"—that is, the second of the two major eras. The writer, then, was noting that the final age had been ushered in. Ever since Jesus' birth, prophecy had been and was being fulfilled. So even in this brief term, the writer made an important claim. The Jews had been waiting for the final age. The writer declared that it had arrived.

The writer's first purpose in the book of Hebrews was to demonstrate to the readers how and why Jesus was and is greater than even prophets or angels. Angels are servants and companions of God, but their status cannot be compared to Christ's. The prophets spoke the Word of God well, as did the angels, but with the advent of the new covenant, God used a far superior mouthpiece: his Son, Jesus Christ.

Jesus is a better spokesman for God because he *is* God. This must be clear from the outset of the epistle, because it is the foundation of the letter's discourse. The deity and supremacy of Christ are primary subjects. Even in just these first four verses we find Jesus' status outlined. We read who he is in relationship to God, the universe, human beings, and angels.

NOT A LESSER MEMBER OF THE TRINITY
(HEB. 1:2)

At first glance, one may think that the first few verses of Hebrews portray Jesus as a lesser member of the Trinity, subservient to God the Father. Nothing could be further from the truth. Rather, the description given identifies Jesus' role within the Trinity, and the intersection of his role as human with his role as God.

The first complication is that he is referred to as "heir." When we think of an heir, we think of someone who is the recipient of someone else's treasure. The heir didn't earn it; he got it because he was the son of someone who had it first. But looking at the rest of verse 2, why does that situation not apply here?

Donald Guthrie writes: "In human affairs the eldest son is the natural heir. In the analogy [in this verse] a more profound thought is introduced. The heir is also the creator. He is not inheriting what he has not been connected with. He inherits what he himself made."[1]

The verse hearkens back to Psalm 2:8: "Ask me, and I will make the nations your inheritance, the ends of the earth your possession." What are the similarities between the two verses? What is the key difference?

Peter O'Brien writes: "The oracle in the psalm echoes Genesis 17:5, where the inauguration of Abraham as heir marks a significant step in redemptive history."[2] The first era began when Abraham, in covenant with God, inherited all nations. The second era is signified by Jesus Christ becoming heir to all that exists.

"Through whom also he made the universe" is a pretty curious statement. We've already discussed that Jesus is heir of what he himself has created, but it isn't the role we usually think of for the Son of God. Savior, not Creator, is the first thing that comes to mind. However, it has been declared elsewhere in Scripture that he is Creator. Take a moment to look up John 1:3 and Colossians 1:16. What do you think it means that God the Father made the universe *through* Jesus the Son? Do you think it matters?

Guthrie says: "The Christians were convinced that the same person who had lived among men was the one who created men."[3] The recipients of Hebrews had not seen Jesus, but many of them had walked the earth when he did. We know that Immanuel means "God with us," and God is with us even today. But for the people of that time, God's presence was palpable. The readers of the letter may have known people who had been with Jesus. God had been with them in such a real sense that they could reach out and touch him. And this Jesus—this man who had walked among them—was the same One who had created them!

Just as ancient Greeks gave much consideration to wisdom, so the Jews reflected upon the wisdom of God. In fact, in passages such as Proverbs 8:22–31, divine wisdom is personified and is said to be God's companion in the creation of the universe.[4] It seems that some Christians began to identify Christ as the living, breathing "Divine Wisdom." The author of Hebrews paws at "wisdom theology" as a cat paws at a dangling string. But in wisdom theology, divine wisdom's personification is still quite mystical, never becoming flesh, never affecting salvation. The author of Hebrews, on the other hand, emphasized that Christ is quite real, quite earthy. While he is the exalted Son of God, he is also the man who walked among us.[5]

REFLECTION QUESTIONS

1. Note that the writer of Hebrews wrote that the prophets spoke "to our ancestors" (Heb. 1:1). Why do you think he said their writings were for people of the past? Why were the ancient prophets still so revered by the Jews during the days of early Christianity?

2. Within the following parallel passages, what are some of the prophecies that were fulfilled, indicating that the final age had begun?

- Isaiah 7:14 and Matthew 1:22–23
- Genesis 49:10 and Luke 3:33

- Isaiah 53:3 and John 7:5–7
- Psalm 34:20 and John 19:33–36
- Psalm 16:10 and Matthew 28:2–7

3. What is Jesus' position in the Trinity (Heb. 1:3)?

4. What is Jesus' relationship to the universe (v. 2)?

5. What is his relationship to the angels (v. 4)?

6. What is his human form (v. 3)?

7. What is his relationship to us? What did he do for us? (v. 3)?

8. As you've read and reflected about the author's description of Christ, what have you learned about who he is? How have you looked at the nature of Christ in a new way?

9. Why is Christ a superior communicator of God's message? Does this mean there is better access to God for those of us who live in the era of Christ, as opposed to those who lived in the days of only the Law and the Prophets?

10. How do you think your relationship with God is different as a Christian than it would have been if you'd been an everyday Israelite in the times of the prophets? Do you think the everyday Israelites experienced intimacy with God?

11. When you think of who Christ is, what do you think your response to him should be today?

WHO CHRIST IS, PART 2

HEBREWS 1:3

RADIATING GLORY

When something radiates, it sends out light from a central source. As a sunray is both of the light yet separate from it, Jesus is one with the Father, emanates from the Father, and yet is distinct in his person. God's glory was witnessed on earth because of Jesus' humanity and sojourn among us (John 1:14). It was witnessed in every miracle he performed, in the transfiguration (Matt. 17:1–2), and in the message of love, forgiveness, and freedom he brought.

There's a poetic symbolism when we use rays of light as an illustration. We all need the sun for our survival; we need its light and its warmth. But it is too far, too bright, too hot—we cannot reach up and grab the sun. The beams that radiate its light solve our problem. They bring us the light and warmth we need without burning us. Just as a ray of the sun reaches down from its source to the earth below, Christ reaches down and overcomes the colossal divide between God and man. While being God himself, he stretched down and met us where we are—all the while sparing us from viewing his full *shekinah*[1] glory, which is too brilliant for human beings to behold. As Christ shines upon us, he reveals the glory of God and bathes us in it.

THE "EXACT REPRESENTATION OF HIS BEING"

Have you ever tried to prove that God is triune (three distinct but united persons[2]) by using Scripture alone? It isn't easy. One of my teenage sons recently said to me, "Mom, I've been reading my Bible every day, and I just don't find any evidence that Jesus is God. But I know it is important to believe that."

He was right—it is important to believe that. Since the days of the Nicene Council (AD 325), belief in a triune God has been considered a nonnegotiable for true Christians. But it's no surprise that my son couldn't find evidence of it. The doctrine of the Trinity is sort of the New Testament's breath— essential and consistent, but often indistinguishable.

In the days of the early church, a heretical doctrine was afoot known as "adoptionism." This was the theory that

Jesus Christ was just a man, but God had "adopted" him as his Son. In other words, he was not divine in nature. The role of Messiah was placed upon him at some point during his life, perhaps during his baptism. In his book *Heresies: Heresy and Orthodoxy in the History of the Church*, Harold O. J. Brown admits, "Much of the New Testament can be read in an adoptionist sense; the number of passages that clearly emphasize the deity and preexistence of Christ are few."[3]

The first chapter of Hebrews may seem to have the ring of adoptionism. Verse 4 says, "He became as much superior to the angels." Verse 5 says, "Today I have become your Father." (These verses will be explored in devotion 3.) But perhaps most troublesome is verse 3, which refers to Christ not as God, but as the "exact representation" of God.

Representation seems to indicate a substitute, something less than the actual thing. Imagine that the president was invited to speak at a particular event, but because his schedule was full, he sent another person to represent him. The person may speak the ideas of the president, but he isn't actually the president. In fact, in terms of his position, he is someone less than the president. If Jesus, similarly, was only a representative on behalf of God, wasn't he less than God? How was he any better than the prophets or the angels?

Considering the following illustration may be helpful.

Imagine that you need to paint a small room in your home, so you go to a hardware store to get a gallon of paint.

You choose a card that has a picture of the paint on it and give it to the person who does the paint mixing. "I'd like this color, 'Daylight Blue,'" you say.

"Come back in fifteen minutes," the mixer tells you.

You go and shop around a bit. While you are gone, the employee mixes the paint. But before he seals the lid on your gallon of paint, he dips a paint stick in the paint. Then he puts a dollop of that paint on the lid and seals it.

When you return, your gallon of paint is sealed, but there on the top is an *exact representation* of your Daylight Blue paint. You can't see the whole gallon. But you know the true color and consistency and brightness of that paint because of the representation on top. It is an exact representation because it is the same stuff that is in your can. To use more theological terms, it is *of the same essence* as the paint in the can. It is *in very nature* the same as the paint in the can. But because it isn't the entire gallon of paint, we say that it *represents* the paint inside.

You are pleased with the representation on the can. You notice, however, that it doesn't look exactly the same as the color on the card. (It never does!) You notice that the actual paint is brighter, bluer, or glossier. Just as the card is an imperfect representation of the paint color and substance, so were the angels and prophets imperfect representations of God and his message. And just as the dollop of paint on the sealed lid is the exact representation of the unseen paint in the can, so Christ Jesus is the exact representation of the Godhead.

The phrase that is translated as "exact representation" in the NIV is worded as "exact imprint" in the *New Revised Standard Version*, which may be more helpful. When Hebrews was written, coins bore the images of the rulers, just as our coins have images of important persons in the history of our country. The idea of an "exact representation" would have meant to the congregation that Jesus bore the imprint of God himself, just as a Roman coin bore the imprint of Caesar.

THE WRITER'S MYSTERIOUS ANGLE

Despite all of this, one may wonder why the author wasn't more forthright. Why didn't he just say that Jesus is God and be done with the matter? Why did he have to be mysterious about it?

Let's consider what our writer was establishing in Hebrews 1. It is clear that he wanted to present a hierarchy, and he did so by defining relationships. Who is Jesus in relationship to man? Who is he in relationship to angels? Who is he in relation to God the Father? This would be of vital importance to early Christians. So while we may be looking for the passage to bluntly tell us there is a Trinity and Jesus Christ is the second person of that Trinity, the writer does so in a more subtle way. He knew his culture and he understood the times. He needed to show the superiority of Christ as representative of God, and he did it in a way that the ancient believers would easily understand. We may wish he had spoken directly to his twenty-first-century audience, answering our specific questions. But he didn't.

Don't be disheartened! Really searching for what the Scriptures teach us is a great joy. If everything were completely obvious, if there were never any clues to hunt down or revelations to tease out, we might not become as intimate with God's Word. As it is, we have to work to understand it. As we invest our time and engage our brains, we dwell in God's presence and we digest what God has to say, rather than gloss over it.

"SUSTAINING ALL THINGS BY HIS POWERFUL WORD"

Let us try to imagine the weight of this claim in the context of the first century. If the new believers had grown up in the Jewish faith, would they have been rattled to read the claim that Jesus, the man who walked among them, sustains all things? That his word is as powerful as the word of God the Father? What a bold, unabashed case was being made for the authority of Jesus Christ!

We must not miss the fact that while the writer did not bluntly assert, "Jesus is God," he was emphatically stating so by declaring that the powerful word of Jesus sustains the universe. If indeed the recipients were raised as Jews, they would have understood the point. And if they were raised as Hellenists, they would have understood that this would set Jesus up as higher than any god in their society's religious structure.

The second doctrine of The Salvation Army says: "We believe that there is only one God, who is infinitely perfect, the Creator, Preserver, and Governor of all things, and who is the only proper object of religious worship."[4] In Hebrews 1:2, the writer named Jesus as Creator. Now in verse 3, he was claiming Jesus as Preserver and Governor.

WHEN JESUS SAT DOWN

The book of Hebrews was written so that everyone might understand that the new sin sacrifice and the new High Priest were complete and perfect. The animal sacrifices and the human priests of the past were temporary solutions to the sin problem and not fully sufficient. Jesus Christ—the established Creator, Preserver, and Governor—made the final and complete sacrifice. When we understand who he really is, we can understand why his sacrifice was enough.

John MacArthur writes,

The marvelous thing about this statement is that Jesus, the perfect High Priest, sat down. This is in great contrast to the priestly procedure under the Old Covenant. There were no seats in the tabernacle or the temple sanctuaries. The priest had no place to sit because God knew it would never be appropriate for him to sit. His responsibility was to sacrifice, sacrifice, sacrifice, over and over again. So the priests offered sacrifices daily—and never sat down. But Jesus offered one sacrifice, and said, "It is finished."[5]

REFLECTION QUESTIONS

1. The image of light radiating from a source is a strong one. What insight do you have about Christ radiating God's glory? How does this imagery speak to you?

2. Why do you think it matters that Christ was actually God incarnate, rather than just a man who grew up to become the Christ?

3. What do these terms mean in general and specifically about Christ: *creator*, *preserver*, *governor*?

4. How was the writer subtly building a case that Jesus is God?

5. Give a description of Christ, bearing in mind the things we've read about him in Hebrews 1:3.

6. When you consider who Christ really is, and how this almighty One was willing to make himself the sacrifice for us, do you feel prompted to clear your heart before him? Ask him to examine you and reveal any sinful ways. Are you prepared to give them up as you stand in the light of our radiant Savior?

3

CHRIST OVER THE ANGELS

HEBREWS 1:4–14

SUPERIOR NAME (HEB. 1:4–5)

The previous devotion could have included verse 4, because it is the conclusion of the introductory declaration at the beginning of Hebrews 1. Indeed, many studies of Hebrews make a division between verses 4 and 5, not 3 and 4. But verse 4 also serves as the start to the passage that compares Christ and angels. As a conclusion to the introduction, it makes the case that Christ was superior to angels, just as he was superior to prophets. But as the start of the next passage, the writer essentially claimed, "Christ is far above the angels. Now I will prove it."

The superior name Jesus inherited is "Son." It is possible that some of the recipients of the letter considered Jesus to be an angel or something much like an angel. It is possible that the writer of Hebrews was trying to suppress the notion that Jesus was the same as an angel by proving he is something *better than* an angel.

Angels were so esteemed that some people actually worshiped them. Even if the readers did not think of Jesus as an angel, the prevailing understanding of the times was that the Old Testament law had been given to Moses by an angel that served as mediator (see Acts 7:38 and Gal. 3:19). This is one of the reasons the Jews regarded angels so highly.

THE SON OF GOD (HEB. 1:5–13)

In verses 5–13, we find a series of quotes from the Old Testament. The quotes found in verses 5–6 hearken back to what was written about the kings in David's family line. For example, the two quotes in verse 5 are taken from Psalm 2:7 and 2 Samuel 7:14. They constituted the word from God delivered to a king through a prophet, and they were meant to celebrate the coronation of the new king.

But there was some understanding that, in the larger sense, these promises would ring true throughout the centuries (for all the Davidic kings) and would eventually describe the Messiah King, who would also be a descendant of David. So while a human king was loftily called the "son" of God, the title was always meant to point toward Jesus.

Understanding that these verses originally described human kings, we can understand why there would be phrases such as "I have become your Father" (Heb. 1:5). For certainly God did not *become* the father of Jesus Christ. The relationship was always there. Even so, scholars have asked what it means that God has said, "Today I have become your father" (v. 5). What day is considered "today"?

In the human application of the psalm, "today" would have been the day a man became king—his coronation day. Similarly, in the case of Jesus, "today" is the day that he was exalted, having completed his work, and took his place at God's right hand. Of course, he was always the Son of God. *Word Biblical Commentary* says that Jesus was once the "pre-existent Son" (before coming to earth), then the "incarnate Son" (in the flesh), and finally the "exalted Son." The exalted Son had completed his mission to live as a human, die, and rise again. Having done so, "he entered into a new dimension in the experience of sonship."[1]

THE REIGNING ONE (HEB. 1:5–13)

In verses 5–13, the author used Old Testament quotes as support for the claims Hebrews 1:2–3 makes about Jesus. Here are the claims with their back-up verses:

- 2b: Christ was appointed heir of all things. Verses 5–9, quoting Psalm 2:7; 2 Samuel 7:14; Deuteronomy 32:43; Psalm 104:4; 45:6–7: Son and heir who reigns over all forever.
- 2c: The universe was created through Christ. Verse 10, quoting Psalm 102:25: credits Jesus for establishing the heavens and the earth.
- 3a, b: Christ is God (see previous devotion), and he is eternal. Verses 10–12, quoting Psalm 102:25–27: eternal and unchanging.
- 3c: Christ has ascended to his place of exaltation at the right hand of God. Verse 13, quoting Psalm 110:1: God the Father has welcomed him to his right hand.

THEN WHAT ABOUT THE ANGELS? (HEB. 1:14)

After (hopefully) fully convincing his audience that Christ is superior to angels, the author polished off his point by stressing that the role of an angel is to minister and serve. This reads as though the job is twofold: ministering in heaven at the throne of God and serving humankind, the inheritors of salvation.

REFLECTION QUESTIONS

1. Can you think of biblical incidents that might have helped build the reputation of angels, both in the Jewish community and in the community of new Christians (for example, Ex. 33:1–3; Matt. 2:13)?

2. Why do you think the author of Hebrews referred to Scripture that had to do with human kings?

3. If Jesus went from "pre-existent Son" to "incarnate Son" to "exalted Son," does that imply a change in the essence of who he is? Can God change roles without changing his nature?

4. When you think of Jesus, do you envision him more as the incarnate Son who walked this earth or the exalted Son who is seated beside the Father?

5. All of the claims about Jesus Christ are critical. But are one or two of them more important or more moving or more surprising to you personally? Why or why not?

6. Describe the relationship between God the Father and God the Son based solely on Hebrews 1:5–13.

7. Read Philippians 2:6–11. Jesus, too, came to serve humankind! But how does his role as servant differ from an angel's role?

8. After describing Jesus as an heir to God, the author referred to *us* as heirs of salvation. Since the author did nothing carelessly, what was he trying to establish by calling

us "those who will inherit salvation" (Heb. 1:14)? How does this link us to Christ and distinguish us from angels?

9. What do you think our general perception of angels is today? How does it differ from the view ancient Jews had?

10. In this devotion, we looked at how the author used Old Testament verses to support his claims about Christ. We may never know for certain who wrote Hebrews, but we can easily see that the book was carefully and skillfully constructed. Hebrews is lauded for its logic, tightly knit arguments, and rhetoric. What role do your intellectual skills play in your life as a Christian?

4

THE GREAT SALVATION AND ITS RECIPIENTS

HEBREWS 2:1–4

THE DRIFTERS (HEB. 2:1)

In the past three devotions, we've seen the author of Hebrews verify the lordship of Jesus Christ. We have studied how superior Jesus is to the prophets and angels, who first carried God's message to humankind. The author has therefore established the groundwork to admonish his readers at the beginning of Hebrews 2. If the first covenant was mighty, and the prophets and angels were God's veritable mouthpieces, then how much greater is the new covenant, the great salvation—paid for and delivered to us by the Son of God himself? How dare we ignore what Christ has provided?

Drifters aren't those who intentionally turn their backs to God. Drifting is a gradual process. Think about when you mark your spot on a beach by laying out your chair, towel, or cooler. Then you get into the water and play for a while. When you return to the sand, you discover that your things are not close by. You have not exited the water at the same place you entered it. While you were unaware, the current of the water caused you to drift.

Even if the drifting is unintentional, it is quite serious. It may have been caused by mere carelessness, but carelessness is nothing to be taken lightly. Let's say I have something I must do, so I leave my younger children with a babysitter. But while they are there, the sitter decides to leave them and run to the store. She has no malicious intent; she's just unbelievably careless. Does that make it OK? If one of them were to have an accident while she was gone, would that make the injury any less severe?

Perhaps it is even easier for us to be careless with the gospel than it was for the first Christians. Many of us grew up in church and even in Christian homes. We heard Scripture all the time. One of my children once said, "You're going to read the Bible to us again? But I already know everything in it!"

Even if you didn't grow up in a family of faith, you likely caught on to what some of the basics of Christianity are just by reading, watching television, and being part of the world. The long-running, popular American sitcom *The Big Bang Theory* provides an illustration. The scientists around whom the show is centered spend three months at the North Pole trying to prove some aspect of string theory.

When they get home, one of the men's mothers, who is characterized as a devout Christian, calls to check on him. We hear Sheldon say, "No, Mother, I didn't feel your prayer group praying for me. No, Mother, I don't think that my safe return proves that it worked."

Why is that (supposedly) funny? Because viewers have all heard of prayer groups. They've heard that kind of lingo and know it well enough to understand when it's mocked.

Of course, this society-wide familiarity with religion is rapidly changing. We are told we now live in a post-Christian era. Many young adults have grown up without even a passing familiarity with Christianity. We are at a very dangerous point in history. It is not new that many people of faith have heard the Word of God over and over but have never developed a passion for it. It is not new that Christians are vulnerable to drifting. But twenty-first-century drifting may get us off course further than ever before, because now we live in an environment that is ceasing to make reference to God at all. People live moral, good, generous lives *without* a spiritual compass. We cannot afford to be careless with the gospel, or we will soon convince ourselves there is no need for it. How long will it take for Christianity to be nothing more than a sentimental relic?

THE IGNORERS (HEB. 2:2–3)

"The message spoken through angels" (v. 2) and the punishment for its violation is a reference to the cautionary story of the Israelites under Moses. The Israelites were often disobedient in their trek from Egypt to Canaan. But it came to a head when they reached the Promised Land and refused to go in, afraid they could not conquer the people already living there (Num. 13–14). God then forbade entrance to an entire generation, waiting until they died off before their children could enter.

God had proved his saving power when he led them out of Egypt. But that wasn't enough for the Israelites. And the binding message that had been delivered was of no consequence. As a result, they never entered the Promised Land.

The salvation of the people under Moses was, for the purposes of the book of Hebrews, earthbound. But not so with this new "great salvation." As chapter 2 of Hebrews progresses and we move into chapters 3 and 4, we get a picture of the fullness of this salvation. It involves "the world to come," of which Jesus is the ruler. It also includes our coming "Sabbath rest"—not just a break on Saturday or Sunday, but the eternal rest that God will grant to Christ's followers. The author of Hebrews always had his eye on what is future, what is eternal.

What, then, will be the punishment for those who refuse to submit themselves to the perfect salvation provided by Christ? If the first punishment was being turned away from the Promised Land, can we conclude that ignoring this better covenant means being turned away from heaven, a kind of eternal Promised Land?

Some say that "ignoring" the great salvation implies something intentional unlike the careless "drifting" of verse 1.[1] The interesting thing is that, either way, the text is addressed to "we"—specifically to believers. Let me make my point clear: The indication is that someone who is a believer may very well drift or consciously turn from one's faith. Many Christians do not believe that salvation can be lost once it has been accepted. This passage is problematic for those who hold that understanding. But it is a persuasive verse for those of us who see salvation as something that can be forsaken. Do notice, however, that *God* doesn't take back his saving grace. Whether one drifts or departs, it is one's own action, not God's.

SIGNS AND WONDERS (HEB. 2:4)

The previous salvation plan was announced through angels (v. 2). The new plan is announced through the Lord himself. The mention of signs and wonders may have reminded the original readers that God used signs and wonders during the exodus from Egypt to show his power and to show who his true people were (for example see Ex. 7:3–5). Now, the Holy Spirit uses the same technique to prove the truth of Christ's message and who his new people are. This consistent parallelism, which we have seen and will continue to see in Hebrews, seems to be a purposeful tool.

In the early days of Christianity, things could be fairly dramatic — signs, wonders, displays of gifts of the Spirit. Acts 19:1–7 is a great example. Paul met some Ephesians who had received John's baptism only, and had never heard of the Holy Spirit. The baptism John offered only pointed to the coming Christ and demanded repentance. So Paul introduced them to the completed work of Jesus Christ. He laid hands on them and they received the Holy Spirit. This resulted in immediate prophesying and speaking in tongues!

Surely God affirmed the establishment of the new covenant with spectacular things. But the Holy Spirit hasn't left us. God's miraculous power hasn't dried up. Perhaps when we pray, we should expect more. As the children's song says:

> God's not dead — no! He's still alive!
> God's not dead — no! He's still alive!
> God's not dead — no! He's still alive!
> I feel him all over me!

Do we feel him all over us?

REFLECTION QUESTIONS

1. In verse 1, what do you think the author was referring to when he wrote, "What we have heard"? How do we pay attention to it?

2. The inattentive believer is surrounded by "currents" that cause drifting. What do you encounter in this world that might cause a believer—maybe yourself, specifically—to drift? What can be done to avoid those things?

3. How is our world different now that we are in the postmodern, post-Christian age?

4. Do you believe a person can lose his or her salvation? Would simply drifting do that, or would it have to be a conscious decision?

5. What point is driven home through the comparison between the experience of those who followed Moses and those who follow Christ?

6. Have you ever witnessed a miracle or some sort of sign or wonder? What happened?

7. What gifts of the Holy Spirit have you seen at work around you?

8. What gifts has the Holy Spirit given to you? How are you using them?

5

CHRIST HUMBLED AND EXALTED

HEBREWS 2:5–9

UNDERSTANDING WHO JESUS WAS AND IS

When my oldest son was a young boy, Bill Clinton, who was the sitting United States president at the time, came to our city to give a public address. I wanted my son to have the chance to see a president in person, so we attended the event. I thought it was a great, patriotic opportunity, but I'm not quite sure what it was like from the perspective of a seven-year-old. He knew that he was seeing someone of status, and the crowd of thousands must have communicated that this was a big deal. He had certainly learned about the office of the president at school, but he didn't have enough experience to understand the significance of that role.

I think the disciples of Jesus—not just the Twelve, but all of them—must have felt the same way. When his life, death, and resurrection were completed, I can imagine they stood back and said, "Exactly what just happened here? I'm not sure I grasp the full meaning."

Hebrews is such an important book because, among other things, it gives us such a full picture of the divine/human nature of Jesus, his salvific (saving) work, his ongoing role as high priest/mediator, and his eternal status. If any early believer was still scratching his or her head about what the coming and leaving of Christ had meant, the epistle of Hebrews would have been a prime resource. Hebrews explained the man who had recently been on earth and the power of what he'd done.

In Hebrews 2:5–9, the author described the humiliation of Christ and his subsequent exaltation. But let us not forget that our writer was a technical master. He used Psalm 8, a psalm about humankind, to help us understand the ultimate human—Jesus Christ.

Before we explore this quote from the Psalms, we simply can't ignore the unusual phrase: "But there is a place where someone has testified" (Heb. 2:6). One may wonder if the writer of Hebrews was a bit lazy. Didn't our writer recognize this as Psalm 8? And if not, couldn't he have done a little research?

The writer did not leave out the specifics because of ignorance; it was intentional. "Precisely because it is God who speaks in the [Old Testament], the identity of the person through whom he uttered his word is relatively unimportant."[1] By citing neither psalmist nor reference, the writer made sure we focus on the original Source. He continued to do this throughout the book.

The quote from Psalm 8 almost feels like sleight of hand. The author took a passage that is a known celebration of humanity, and used it to point to the Savior. How and why has the writer repurposed the psalm like this?

Hebrews 2:5 tells us: "It is not to angels that he has subjected the world to come." We know from Hebrews 1 that Jesus is the one to whom the coming world will be subjected. We must reframe the psalm—which speaks of the subjection of the world—to think in terms of Jesus rather than his creation.

Second, in the Old Testament, the title "son of man" was used to refer to a person. It is repeatedly found as a reference to Ezekiel, for example. But in the New Testament, it refers to the God-man, Jesus. The writer used the title now to emphasize Jesus' humanity.

Third, it was the original plan for humans to rule the earth, but we sinned and lost our authority. In the perfected world to come, however, the "second Adam," as Jesus is called, will rule forever. Cockerill explains it like this:

The preacher's [the writer of Hebrews] ambiguity is probably intentional. In the first place, he is speaking about humanity. Although Psalm 8 describes the exalted place given to humanity in God's creation, humanity has fallen into sin. . . . Certainly humanity has fallen short of the great salvation which God has provided and of dwelling in God's presence in the heavenly homeland. But the psalm also applies to Jesus, as Hebrews 2:9 makes clear. He is the man par excellence, the representative of humanity. He is the One who, as a man, will enable humanity to fulfill the destiny to which the psalm points."[2]

As the only one worthy of fulfilling the destiny of man in Psalm 8, we see that Jesus perfects and completes God's original plan, rather than reinvents it.

THE HUMILITY OF JESUS (HEB. 2:8–9)

In Hebrews 1, the writer took great pains to prove the superiority of Christ over the angels. Having wrapped our minds around that, it is impactful to read that he was temporarily made lower than they. It is even more stunning to think that he became just like you and me.

Undercover Boss is an American television reality show that has gained great popularity. In each episode, the CEO of a true-life major corporation takes on one of the lowest positions in the company. The people who are lower in the ranks have never seen the CEO, so they don't recognize him or her. There's something touching about the idea of the big boss experiencing the menial jobs firsthand. Unlike human bosses, though, Jesus could have understood what it meant to be human without actually becoming human. He is God; he knows all. But *we* are moved and encouraged because we know that he actually walked in our shoes. We understand two things from his humble act: (1) he knows what it is to be one of us, and (2) he would do anything — *anything* — to reach us.

A GLORIFIED JESUS (HEB. 2:9)

The coming of the kingdom brings the tension of "already, but not yet." Jesus' mission on earth inaugurated the kingdom of God, but there is so much that we are still waiting for. Yes, Christ is King, everything is subject to him . . . but we don't see that yet. It is already a fact, in the sense that there is no question that someday every knee will bow and every tongue confess that Jesus Christ is Lord. Yet, we wait. In the meantime, his people need to acknowledge him as King in their own lives and in the church. We must crown him with glory and honor now.

AND THE POINT WAS . . . (HEB. 2:9)

After painting a clear picture of who Christ is and who he was on earth, we come to something of a climax in verse 9 when the author described the critical work of the Savior. Not only did he leave his heavenly place, not only did he debase himself, but he did what is almost unthinkable: He suffered and died for our sakes.

And here is where you and I could easily ignore the great salvation message. Yes, we know he died for our sins. We've heard it more times than we can count. Those who saw the movie *The Son of Man* or the television series *The Bible* may have felt a temporary stirring in their hearts as they viewed reenactments of the crucifixion. But it can be very hard to be moved over and over by the same thing.

We have taken considerable time moving through Hebrews 1 and 2. Perhaps dwelling in these verses, really looking at who Christ is, can make our hearts jump once again when we read that by the grace of God he tasted death for us.

I am a very poor artist. We're talking stick figures at best. But at a point like this, I find it helpful to draw a picture of Christ at his loftiest, and then meditate on what he abandoned for our sakes and how he was humbled. I would never share my simple pictures with anyone, not even my husband, but they help me connect with God.

Can you think of something that would help you focus on the grandeur of Christ and the enormity of his sacrifice? Maybe you'd like to write a poem or draw a picture or even write a song. Write this in your journal or notebook.

REFLECTION QUESTIONS

1. Perhaps Christ could have sacrificed himself for our sin without spending thirty-three years as a human. Does it make a difference to you that he lived the human life? Why?

2. There is a cause-and-effect relationship between Christ's earthly sacrifice and being crowned with glory. If Christ was already divine, why do you think he was crowned with glory after his work was done?

3. Take a moment to reflect on the majesty of Jesus Christ as he is now, exalted after his resurrection. Write a prayer of adoration.

4. In the case of Christ, his position as lower than the angels was a temporary one. In what way do you think he was "lower" when on earth?

5. What was the purpose in Christ being humbled like this?

6. Consider whether there may be any aspect of your life you have yet to bring under his authority. Are you ready to let him be King of all?

7. How do you think the sin of our first parents prevented us from fulfilling our destiny? How did Christ step in and complete the picture?

8. God's original design for human beings was pretty spectacular. We were created in his image! How does freedom in Christ give us the power to become something better than what we were before we were saved? Is this only about living a pure life, or can we become more creative, more joyful, more intuitive, more confident—in short, can we look more similar to God? What part of you could be more like God?

6

ESTABLISHING US AND OUR FAITH

HEBREWS 2:10–18

PARTICIPANTS IN THE "NEW EXODUS" (HEB. 2:10)

As Moses ushered the Israelites out of Egypt and toward Canaan, Jesus leads us from the bondage of sin and toward glory. Hebrews 2:10 declares that Christ leads "many sons and daughters" on this new exodus. That declaration may sound as though it excludes some people, but it is meant to demonstrate a new sense of inclusion. In the Old Testament, the Lord was mainly the God of the Israelites. Now he is the God of many! Even better, verse 9 identified "many" as "everyone."

THE DEATH THAT PERFECTED (HEB. 2:10)

Jesus pioneered—initiated—our Christian faith, when he died for us. The author wrote that the death that inaugurated this great salvation was "fitting." That would have been an interesting concept for a first-century Jew. The Jews, of course, were well familiar with the horrors of crucifixion. They commonly held that if a person were condemned to such a death, that person was under the curse of God. Perhaps the idea of Jesus dying a cursed death rings true when we remember that he took upon himself the sin of all the world. It is a sobering thought, considering your sin and my sin played a role in his condemnation.[1]

How curious that the author should say that Jesus was made "perfect through what he suffered" (v. 10). Wasn't Jesus already perfect? Looking at the Greek, the original language of the New Testament, the word *perfect* can often be translated as "complete." In today's vernacular, it would be more accurate to say Jesus was made complete through his suffering. Still, that's pretty confusing. Was Jesus somehow incomplete before his death?

The author was leading up to verse 17, where he would reveal to us that Jesus has received the role of high priest. In this role, he had to be able to identify with us in every way. By taking on our sin, experiencing our pain, and submitting himself to the will of the Father, he completed a prerequisite for his new role. The text simply means that Jesus was being made ready for this critical position.

BROTHERS AND SISTERS (HEB. 2:11)

In this context, being "made holy" refers to the status conferred upon us as believers. Just as the high priest's animal sacrifice had made the people presentable before God in the past, now it is the sacrifice of Christ that makes us presentable. His blood consecrates us. And as we are now found suitable before God, Christ claims us as his own brothers and sisters. First, he became human and identified with us in that way. And now, this holy Son of God has made *us* sons and daughters of God—his own brothers and sisters—in an "extended sense," to borrow a phrase from Peter O'Brien.[2]

In the culture of the first readers of Hebrews, *brother* was a significant term. People of equal social status would call each other "brother." If a person of higher or lower status was referred to in that way, it was meant to show unity. While we will never be equal to Christ, he honors us more than we can imagine by calling us his brothers and sisters. It speaks of his solidarity with us. Though he is infinitely above us, he has made himself one of us. Moreover, he wants us to know that this connection will always exist.

THREE QUOTES (HEB. 2:12–13)

As seen in Hebrews 1 (devotion 3), the writer used recognizable Old Testament passages in unexpected ways to further his point.

The first quote comes from Psalm 22. Because this psalm opens with the words Jesus spoke on the cross, believers in Christ realize that Psalm 22 was "messianic," that is, it prophesied the words of the Messiah for whom the Israelites were waiting. If these were undeniably the words of Christ, the author could use them to emphasize that Christ counted us as brothers and sisters.

The second quote is from Isaiah 8:17. Isaiah spoke these words as he waited for God to fulfill his word, even though the people to whom he prophesied were unbelieving. Eventually, Isaiah saw the rise of a remnant of faithful Israelites. By applying these words to Jesus, the author emphasized Jesus' trust and endurance, and it is Jesus who leads an uprising of faithfulness.

The third quote is from Isaiah 8:18. Isaiah referred to himself and his biological children, but in this context we think of Jesus and his followers, especially if we remember Jesus' prayer in John 17. God the Father has given to Jesus all those who would respond to his call.

When we read, "the children God has given me" (Heb. 2:13), we need not interpret this to mean that God chooses who will and will not be saved. Think of it this way. Imagine you own a football team. With a generous heart, you invite any and every football player to be on that team. Come one, come all. The invitation is open, but not everyone accepts. Then, if you were to sell the team to someone else, that person would acquire all the players who had voluntarily joined it.

God has given the group "believers" to Christ. All people have been invited to join the group, but it is our choice whether we do or not.

THE POINT OF JESUS' HUMANITY (HEB. 2:14–18)

We come to a climax in these verses. Why was Jesus made human? How does it benefit us? He couldn't die if he hadn't become human. By his death he conquered the Devil. By his death he freed those who feared their own death (implied: because he rose from the dead). His humanity made him a merciful, faithful high priest—and the atonement for our sins. The two statements above are not surprising statements based on what we've read already. But then, the author threw in something wonderful, something we haven't heard yet: He can help us through our temptation because he's survived it himself. We will see more on this in Hebrews 4.

REFLECTION QUESTIONS

1. Who was included when Moses led the people out of Egypt?

2. Who is included in the new exodus?

3. How do you understand this idea of being a brother or sister of Jesus Christ?

4. Does being a son or daughter of God make you equal to Christ? What have you read so far in Hebrews that might help you answer that question?

5. In what way was Jesus the pioneer of a new faith?

6. How do the Old Testament quotes in verses 12 and 13 support the author's message?

7. Verse 17 says that Jesus was "fully human in every way." List some things that are a normal part of the human experience—for example, feeling our stomachs growl, spontaneously laughing when we see something funny, stubbing a toe. Spend a moment thinking of our Lord experiencing these things.

PART 2

THE PERFECT
REST

HEBREWS 3–5

7

JESUS: GREATER THAN MOSES, BRINGER OF HOPE

HEBREWS 3:1–6

"FIX YOUR THOUGHTS" (HEB. 3:1)

If we look at the first verse of Hebrews 3 as a transition between what's just been written and what is about to be written, we find two reasons to fix our thoughts on Jesus. First, we've just read that Jesus is able to help us in times of temptation. Every Christian would say that he or she wishes to overcome temptation. Yet, oddly, we often have our eyes glued to what causes temptation! One person might be struggling with his temper, but he plays violent video games. One might be battling lust, yet she watches unrealistic, titillating romance movies.

Second, the author was about to prove Jesus' superiority over Moses. For the original readers, the message would be, "Don't keep looking to Moses as the great one. Fix your eyes on the One we now understand to be our apostle and high priest."

In our day, there may be other people we are tempted to revere. For those concerned with their spiritual growth, they may miscast their eyes on a great preacher rather than on the One the preacher is preaching about. We may also be tempted to fix our eyes on those we think are exceptionally bright or talented, such as heroes of the entertainment world or of the intellectual world.

JESUS, MOSES, AND THE HOUSE (HEB. 3:2–6)

Remember that for thousands of years the Hebrews had revered Moses as the greatest man who had ever lived. Imagine how it had been drilled into the head of every Jewish child, and how it had been emphasized to each Jewish convert. The covenant between God and man had come through Moses; how could any man be more significant than Moses? Making the case for Jesus' superiority was crucial if the people were to understand that he actually was God. Here, the author used a house as an illustration to demonstrate how Jesus outranks Moses.

Jesus is greater than Moses, just as the builder of a house is greater than the house itself. Jesus is identified as the builder. The next sentence says God is the builder of everything. Once again the point is made that Jesus is Creator (1:2), Jesus is God, equal to the Father. Moses was a faithful servant in the house. The message he delivered was meant to point us to the future covenant. The complex dual role of Christ is seen again (similar to the creator/heir role in chapter 1). He built the house, yes. But here he is portrayed as the Son of the owner-builder, God the Father. As a son, he manages the household (3:6). Obviously, a son is greater than a servant.

BEING THE HOUSE (HEB. 3:6)

The original readers—and us today—play a role in this illustration as well. We are the house. Or, it may make more sense to think of ourselves as the household, the people who are at home in that space, the people who belong.

But verse 6 declares that we are his house if we remain constant. As God speaks through the book of Hebrews, he stresses the importance of our continued faith in him. The verse seems to indicate that should we let go, we will not be members of the house.

As members of the household, we firmly grasp two things. First, our "confidence." The Greek word used for *confidence* describes the freedom that citizens had with their government, including the freedom of speech. What a beautiful idea to apply to our relationship with God and our position in his house! The work of Christ has made us equally free as members of the house of God.

Second, we hold on to our "hope." "The hearers are to hold fast to God's work for them in Christ, which includes all that has been promised. The realization of these promises is a hope that is yet unseen."[1]

It is important for us to understand that our salvation is not completely precarious. We don't need to worry that if we don't feel hopeful one day that we are no longer saved. The idea is that we don't walk away. We don't abandon the truth that we have come to know.

It might have been easy for the first readers of Hebrews to neglect their newfound confidence before God. In so doing, they would be returning to the familiar ways of Judaism, relying on the priest to intercede for them. The writer warned them not to waver, not to return to what they once knew. This would be a rejection of the new covenant of Christ in favor of the original, temporary covenant of Moses. How wrong this would be! For we know that Christ is greater than Moses. We know that Christ is divine and the eternal ruler in the age to come. We know he brought a new, great salvation. What a mistake it would be to give up the freedom he brought!

It may be easy even today to turn our backs on the hope we have in Christ. On April 15, 2013, two terrorists detonated a bomb near the finish line of the Boston Marathon. Three people were killed, and many more were injured. In response to the event, a popular website called Soul Pancake declared that God had a lot of explaining to do. What kind of God was he to allow that sort of evil in the world?

We might well lose heart. We see more evil than good sometimes. Remember that the kingdom of God is here now, but not in its completeness. We see evidence of the kingdom all around us in nature and in the goodness of his people. Evil still exists; however, it will be eradicated one day. We *hope* in what we cannot see.

REFLECTION QUESTIONS

1. How do we "fix our thoughts on Jesus" in a practical way?

2. What type of people do you tend to admire? How can your admiration be kept in check?

3. Just as Moses was a great servant in God's house, God expects faithful service from us, too. Do you know how God wants you to serve? Are you faithfully doing it?

4. What do you hope for in Christ?

5. How would you answer the accusation on the Soul Pancake website?

8

THE LESSON OF THE ISRAELITES

HEBREWS 3:7–19

WHY GOD WAS ANGRY (HEB. 3:7–11)

Hebrews 3:7–11 quotes Psalm 95:7–11. The passage in Psalms harkens back to the greatest failure of the Israelites after they left Egypt.

For forty years the Israelites wandered. Then, when the Promised Land was in sight, Moses sent spies to see what challenges might await in conquering the inhabitants. Joshua and Caleb returned from the mission confident that the people could conquer in God's strength. The other spies, however, were completely intimidated and brought a negative report.

The people lost heart. Despite all they had seen God do for them, they didn't believe he could finish the job. This unbelief cost an entire generation its future. Instead of living in the wonderful place God had promised to them, they continued to camp in the wilderness. They were a nation without a home until the generation of doubters, with the exception of Caleb and Joshua, died out.

You can almost hear the frustration in God's voice: "For forty years they saw what I did" (Heb. 3:9). The same can be true of us, however. We see God prove his power and his care over and over again, but suddenly we doubt. We grow fearful. Our faith wavers. Some big challenge comes our way, and we think, "Oh no, I'm sunk."

The "rest" this generation never knew was the joy of entering the Promised Land. Forty years of travel—imagine it! On your feet, no less! One can understand how getting to the destination would be described as "rest." What's more, this rest meant they would finally have land with fertile soil, and they wouldn't be thirsty again. They would be home, the home God had chosen.

The people's lack of faith, however, was enough to keep them from their rest.

APPLYING THE LESSON (HEB. 3:12–14)

It was the people of God who had lost faith in the desert, not a tribe of pagans. And here, the writer warned the Christians—the early believers and us—not to become unbelieving and turn from God. We've seen this message before: We must maintain our faith. It is not impossible for us to lose our faith, so a degree of vigilance is required. Let us not make space for sin that will harden our hearts and drive us away.

Notice that we are to encourage each other every day. We should not judge each other, nor neglect to speak of spiritual things.

I love social media. I love it because people say beautiful things to each other that they would find difficult to say in person. I know, of course, that it can be a tool for hideous abuse. But time after time, I have received spiritual encouragement from friends via social media outlets.

I don't know why we don't have more spiritual conversations with each other in person. Unless we've specifically set time aside for accountability or mentoring, we don't tend to fall into conversations of spiritual encouragement.

Here's a challenge: This very day, encourage a brother or sister in the Lord to keep his or her faith strong. It would be ideal if you would do this in person or on the phone! But if not, send an e-mail or make contact using social media. Write the name of that person here: _____

Let's take that challenge a step further. The next time you are socializing with a group of Christian friends, or even just one friend, do your best to take the conversation to a spiritual level. Why wouldn't we, the people of God, be talking about the things of God?

THE RECAP (HEB. 3:15–19)

The remainder of the passage reiterates what the writer already discussed. He drove home three main points: (1) It was the people of God who had angered God; (2) the people's unbelief angered God, and their unbelief amounted to disobedience; and (3) the people suffered the consequences of their unbelief.

The writer strongly warned us against being careless with the gospel (ch. 2). We must be cognizant of the fact that people who know better, people who have experienced God's care and provision in their own lives, are subject to unbelief. And this unbelief is very serious and carries consequences.

We must not think the book of Hebrews presents a constant threat that hangs over our heads. Certainly God comes to us in love and wants us to respond in love. He does not want us to be faithful to him simply because we are afraid not to be. But is it possible that sometimes we focus on God's grace and forgiveness to the exclusion of his expectations of faithfulness and holy living? We all like to talk about how we can never earn God's love, and how he will forgive anything we do. But as Christians, we are saved from our past life and meant to move forward. Why should we be crippled by unbelief? We have been set free from that. We are the brothers and sisters of Christ, those who speak freely before their God, sanctified. Like the Israelites, we risk offending God when we shrink in unbelief.

REFLECTION QUESTIONS

1. Can you think of a time when God did something amazing in your life? What happened?

2. Can you think of a time when your faith wavered since that great display of God's care? Explain why you think this happened.

3. What do you think you may have missed out on because you lacked faith?

4. What sin(s) tempt you most?

5. Why was God angry enough at the Israelites to deny them their rest?

6. Do you think God's punishment was "for their own good," or do you think it was strictly vengeance?

7. Is God angry with you in your moments of unbelief?

8. Do you use God's forgiveness as an excuse to neglect the maturation process for yourself as a Christian? How can you "encourage one another daily" (Heb. 3:13)?

9

THE PROMISE THAT STILL STANDS

HEBREWS 4:1–12

THE EXTENDED OFFER (HEB. 4:1–3)

A couple of years ago our family expanded when we adopted two young children — brother and sister — from the West Indies. Prior to a brief stay in a foster home, the two had lived with their biological mother for the first years of their lives. Our daughter was three-and-a-half and our son was five-and-a-half when their mother gave them to the local government.

I sometimes wonder if their biological mother could see what I see in them. Did she notice her daughter's fierce intelligence? Was she aware of her son's physical prowess and his almost savant-like sense of direction? In other words, did she see the buckets of potential they have? Did she see the promise in them?

Whether she saw it or not, she made the decision to let someone else invest in them. And then the question hung in the air: Will someone take these children full of promise? My husband, our three sons, and I, through God's blessing, entered into the promise of who they are and what they will be. We were afraid, certainly, but we took a leap of faith. I think now of how beautiful, talented, funny, and spirited these children are. I wonder what would have become of them if things had been different.

Just as my children's biological mother had two beautiful promises within her reach, so the Israelites could have embraced a beautiful promise. The promise included a land of milk and honey. Peace. Rest. However, in fear, a whole generation turned their backs to the promise and languished in the desert. Did they understand the beauty of what God had offered them? Did they see the potential?

Under Christ, the offer of rest is extended again. As we have seen the parallels between the Israelites and the new children of God, we've seen that everything Christ offers is newer, fuller, better. He is the better mediator of a superior covenant. And so, while the rest offered to the Israelites was earthly, the rest offered to us goes beyond that. Through Christ, we can enter into God's eternal rest.

REST (HEB. 4:4–10)

God rested when his creative work was done. This doesn't mean he became inactive; it means he acknowledged the completion of what he did. Someday our work will be done, too, and we will enter into his rest. Some theologians believe we will continue to occupy ourselves, ever engaging in new avenues of creativity or "work" throughout eternity. Whether or not that's the case, we can be assured that the troubled labor of this world will be over.

There is an urgency to claim rights to our coming rest, as there is emphasis on the word *today*. Commentator Kevin Anderson explains this urgency: "It is now clear that in [Psalm] 95:7–8 [the verses the author of Hebrews is quoting] God is renewing his offer of rest 'in these last days' (Heb. 1:2). The opportunity is now but must be seized before the final 'Day' approaches (10:25). This is why the preacher urged his readers in 3:13 to warn one another 'daily' . . . 'as long as it is called Today,' so that no one's heart is hardened."[1]

THE PERIL OF UNBELIEF (HEB. 4:11)

We saw in Hebrews 3:18–19 that unbelief is disobedience. And it is faith—the opposite of unbelief—that saves us. It has always been faith. Paul told us that Abraham's faith was credited to him as righteousness. In Romans 3:21–31, we read that it is faith that puts the saving work of Christ into effect in our lives.

We may feel again that there is a sense of threat here. Believe or perish. We twenty-first-century folks bristle at that, perhaps to our detriment. God wants us to understand what is at stake here! "Our author's aim is to awaken a godly fear in his hearers so that they will be aware of the seriousness of their situation and be moved to persevere."[2]

THE POWER OF GOD'S WORD (HEB. 4:12–13)

Initially, these verses may seem out of context with the writer's tight dissertation. However, the power of the Word of God is important here. We have read that the Israelites hardened their hearts because they did not listen to God's voice. They turned a deaf ear to the Word of God.

Will we behave as the Israelites did? No one can remain faithless and enter the rest of God, because the Word of God cannot be fooled. When we stand in the light of God's truth, who we really are will be fully revealed.

I had a friend in high school who could not lie to her parents. That's not because she *would* not tell a lie. The problem was that when she did, her chest and neck would turn bright red. She couldn't get away with anything!

It is the same with us. Let us not think for a moment that God is persuaded by our church involvement or our work at the food bank. The Word of God judges our thoughts and attitudes. It slices right through us. Most of us know how to behave ourselves. That's not a problem. But if people could read our minds, what would they see?

The 2001 movie *Shallow Hal* had an intriguing premise. The main character, Hal, became bewitched in some way so that he saw people on the outside as they really were on the inside. He saw kind and good people as beautiful, and selfish people as ugly. His friend scratched his head when Hal fell in love with an obese, unattractive girl, since Hal had always put such emphasis on physical beauty. Hal didn't understand his friend's confusion. As far as he could tell, the girl was stunning.

And that is the way God sees us. There is nothing beautiful about those who present themselves as very together and very committed if, in their hearts, they harbor bitterness, envy, or selfishness.

What God is ultimately looking for is a fierce trust in him. Does he see that when he looks at you and me?

REFLECTION QUESTIONS

1. Do you think it is possible for God to cease activities such as creating? What do you think it means that God rested?

2. Why is there an urgency about having faith "today" (Heb. 4:7)?

3. How do you feel about encountering this kind of urgency in the Bible? In your church or your Bible study group, is there a sense of urgency? Should there be?

4. What is the consequence of disbelief, according to verse 11?

5. Have you ever had any trouble believing in the gospel of Jesus Christ? If so, how did you overcome your lack of faith?

6. In your own heart and mind, how do you balance the fear of "perishing" with the message of God's love?

7. Chances are you have faith in the largest sense of the word: believing in the death and resurrection of Christ and its saving effect. But doesn't God expect us to have faith in him for every aspect of our lives? Is there an area of your life where you are prone to doubt God's care: finances, health, etc.?

8. Are you turned off by the almost threatening tone of some of the passages in Hebrews? If so, why?

9. Consider God's view of your heart right now. What does he find beautiful? What does he see that is ugly?

10

THE HIGH PRIEST

HEBREWS 4:14—5:10

HOLDING FIRM (HEB. 4:14)

With God's Word able to breach our defenses, we must hold firm to our faith. We understand why—the previous chapter made clear the consequences of faith and faithlessness. Is there anything that might motivate us, however, when we struggle to hold on?

Indeed, we should be buoyed by the fact that our High Priest is the Son of God and a citizen of heaven. Things may have seemed dismal for the Israelites under Moses and Joshua. But how can we be downhearted? *Our* High Priest is not like any other.

OUR HIGH PRIEST HAS "BEEN THERE" (HEB. 4:15)

It is remarkable that our God would prove his solidarity with us by subjecting himself to temptation. If it had not been possible for Jesus to sin, it would not have been genuine temptation. If he had absolutely no desire to sin, it would not have been temptation. But it *was* temptation.

Most readers are familiar with the story of Jesus being tempted in the desert (see Matt. 4). Since he lived a full human life, though, I think it is safe to assume that he faced plenty of other temptations. We may be uncomfortable picturing Jesus as struggling with sin. But what a comfort to know that he did! Isn't it easier to approach him, knowing that he has felt what we feel?

BEFORE THE THRONE (HEB. 4:16)

The Old Testament story of Esther tells how she invited the king to dinner so she might make an appeal for her own life and the lives of her countrymen. It took every ounce of courage she had, because she could have been killed for being so bold with the king—even though she was his wife.

People with power are frightening, especially if they have power over our individual fate. Yet no king can compare in might to Yahweh, the eternal God. No one else holds time, eternity, and the universe in his hand. No one else has created the air we breathe and the grass on which we walk. None other has designed our respective bodies and chosen what talents we would possess. "Angels bow before him, heaven and earth adore him," we rightfully sing.

This is the God we are invited to approach with confidence. This is the second time we've seen this word — *confidence* — and it means the same thing here as it did in 3:6. We are free to express ourselves before God's authority. We have been granted *rights* — not because of any virtue of our own, but because the virtue of Christ is imparted to us. He is not ashamed to call us his brothers and sisters. As such, we may go before the throne of the Father.

YOM KIPPUR (HEB. 5:1–4)

The high priest offered the atonement for sin every year on Yom Kippur, the Day of Atonement. As a sinner himself, he first had to offer a sacrifice for his own sin. Only a purified man could atone for the sins of others. His task was to go through the outer court of the tabernacle, move into the Holy Place, and then proceed to the Most Holy Place. He could enter this chamber only on Yom Kippur. The priest had to work quickly because the glory of the Lord was within the chamber, and it could be borne for only a very brief time. Symbolically, the priest brought all sins before the Lord in this chamber. As he sprinkled blood on the mercy seat, the sins were forgiven. Until next time, next year.

The first man to conduct the holy ceremony was Aaron, Moses' brother. He received very specific instructions for this special day (see Lev. 16).

SON AND PRIEST (HEB. 5:5–10)

Hebrews characterizes Jesus Christ in two ways: as Son and as High Priest. In Hebrews 5:5, the writer brought both roles together as he quoted Psalm 2:7 and 110:4. What we may find unsettling is that God the Father appears to be superior to God the Son. The Father seems to be assigning duties to the Son. Furthermore, when on earth, Jesus was submissive to God. If Jesus is one of three equal persons in the holy Trinity, how can it be that God the Father appointed him to certain tasks or told him what to do?

Of course, we can't fully understand this mystery, and all illustrations fall short. The fact of the matter is that there is only one Trinity. So we can't point to some earthly example and say, "It's just like that." That being said, let me attempt an imperfect illustration.

My husband and I are separate personalities, but as much as two humans can be, we are joined together as one.

We consider ourselves equal partners in our marriage. One does not rule the other. Let's say we decide to take a family vacation. Because my husband excels at trip planning, it would go without saying that he would take the lead. He would pick the driving route and book the hotel. He would also designate certain roles to me. "Amy, please pack the kids' suitcases," he might say. "Amy, you're in charge of snacks for the trip."

In this scenario, being assigned tasks by my husband does not make me inferior to him. We simply fall into particular roles for the sake of our mission. One might even say that my role for the vacation requires a bit of humility. I'll be sleeping where Rob chooses and, since he always does the driving (because I tend to fall asleep), I must submit myself to the breaks he finds appropriate. But I've agreed to this arrangement.

The Trinity was in self-agreement as to how the great salvation would be accomplished. God the Father did not— could not, I daresay—coerce God the Son. The plan could not succeed unless the Son placed his full authority aside (see Phil. 2:6–8). He *willingly* put on humanity. This must be kept in mind when reading this passage.[1]

THE REQUIREMENT OF SUFFERING (HEB. 5:7)

The priestly role of Christ could not be established without suffering. To identify with us, he had to know what it was to struggle and to hurt. As mentioned in a previous devotion, this may have been more for our benefit than anything else. Being God, he was certainly capable of understanding pain and suffering without experiencing it. But his personal struggle both speaks to us of his solidarity and completes the requirement of a high priest.

Verse 7 reminds us of the intimate look we are given into Jesus' pain when he prayed in Gethsemane (Matt. 26:29; Mark 14:36; Luke 22:42). Kevin Anderson says, "It was not an unrighteous prayer, but a human one."[2] Like any of us would, he recoiled at the idea of an excruciating death. Though his prayer comes from the heart of a frightened man, it is holy and submissive. Let's examine it as a model:

1. He acknowledged God's power.
2. He asked God to deliver him from what was about to happen
3. He vowed to put the will of God above his human will.

Notice that the Scripture says, "He was heard." God gave ear to Jesus' agonized prayer, and yet he did not spare him his death. Sometimes we don't understand why God allows us to suffer through great trials. If God would not remove this burden from his Son, what makes us think he will take away our problems? God has his purposes, though we don't always see them. In the case of Jesus, his submission to God's will changed the history of the world.

If you are currently experiencing a difficult situation, bring it before the Lord now. It is fair to ask for help and deliverance—and you may even get it! But can you sincerely end your prayer as Jesus did: "Not what I will, but what you will"?

JESUS' TASK FULFILLED (HEB. 5:8-10)

When we read the phrase "Son though he was" (v. 8), we should remind ourselves that Jesus wasn't just any son. He was both God and man, and would soon return to his throne and be rightfully exalted. The writer had already taken great care in earlier chapters to be sure we would know this.

In his role as Son and High Priest, Jesus was constrained to learn obedience. When I say my son needs to learn obedience, I am reflecting on the fact that he does not always do as he is told. Such was not the case with Jesus. "There is no inference that Jesus was ever disobedient. Rather, Jesus demonstrated his faithfulness to God by passing the test of suffering (2:18; 4:15)."[3] As an equal member of the Trinity, the Son was experiencing obedience for the first time.

As discussed in devotion 6, the idea of Jesus being "made perfect" refers to the fact that through his suffering he completed his requirements for his task. Think of *perfect* in this context as meaning "complete" or "fully equipped." Just as his suffering fully equipped him for the priestly role, it equipped him to be the Savior of the world. His death is what made him "the source of eternal salvation for all who obey him" (5:9).

Remember that as we read through Hebrews 3, it became clear that God equates faith with obedience. Jesus isn't the source of salvation for people who demonstrate obedience by completing some sort of checklist. The obedience he requires is faith—a genuine, passionate faith, not a loosely held faith that can result in careless drifting. His part was to suffer, and our part is to believe. We could have perished for our own sins, but all we have to do is believe. Does that seem too much for God to require?

REFLECTION QUESTIONS

1. We know that being tempted isn't a sin in itself. According to James 1:13–15, when does sin begin?

2. What does Hebrews 4:16 tell us we receive when we go before the throne?

3. Consider something that is a matter of prayer in your life right now. Examine your personal request in light of the three parts of Jesus' prayer. (The second part may not apply.) Do you find yourself trusting and submitting, or is there a bit of work to be done in that regard?

4. How would things have been different if God had taken pity on Jesus and put a stop to his arrest?

5. What has been the greatest suffering of your life that wasn't caused by your personal choices?

6. How would things have been different if God had taken pity on you and spared you your greatest pain?

7. How has access and approach to God changed for human beings since Jesus took on the role of high priest?

8. Write a prayer of gratitude and praise to Christ for his obedience, sacrifice, and role as your High Priest.

11

MOVING PAST WHAT'S ELEMENTARY

HEBREWS 5:11—6:3

HARD OF HEARING (HEB. 5:11)

There's an old joke about a young man who was hired by a board of deacons to pastor their church, based on the impressive trial sermon he delivered. He moved into the parsonage, set up his office, and showed up that first Sunday morning as the new pastor. To the surprise of those who had elected him, he delivered the same sermon again. That was OK, though, since only the board of deacons had heard it. In fact, they were pleased that the entire congregation got to hear that powerful sermon. They needed it!

The pastor quickly got to know his people. On his second Sunday, he delivered the same sermon. The people thought that was odd. It was even odder when he did it again the following Sunday, and the Sunday after that.

Finally, the board of deacons decided something should be said.

"Pastor, you're a fine preacher. But we've noticed that you've delivered the same sermon over and over," the head deacon said.

"Oh, you noticed?"

"Why, yes. We'd like to know when you're going to preach a new one."

"Oh, I see. Well, I figured that as soon as you all started living out this one, I'd move on to something else!"

That little tale reminds me of the frustration of the writer of Hebrews. There was so much more that he wanted to share, especially about the priesthood of Christ. But the people weren't ready to move on. Like infants who can't venture past a milk diet, they couldn't move past the most rudimentary truths of the faith.

MILK DRINKERS (HEB. 5:12–13)

The Hebrews were slow to learn (see 5:11). The writer had already noted in 2:1 and 3:7–8 that they had refused to pay attention to what they had heard. They had been warned that not listening is a slippery slope. In fact, it was the beginning of the end for the generation of Israelites that never entered their rest.

If there is one thing that has disappointed me in my ministry, it has been discovering that many people spend years as churchgoers without really learning the Word of God. Some Christians can tell you the basic plan of salvation, but not much else.

Sadly, many of our brothers and sisters are missing out on so much because they simply don't pay attention. They don't care. They have other priorities. They go to worship band practice but miss Bible study or Sunday school. They read self-help books but don't study their Bibles. They may even be glancing at Facebook on their smartphones during the Sunday sermon.

In short, they are still sucking down milk, when they should be feasting on sirloin.

MEAL EATERS (HEB. 5:14)

A baby doesn't move from milk to fried chicken in a day. The parents move the child through several stages. After milk comes baby oatmeal. Then there's juice and pureed peas. Eventually, the baby moves into finger cereal and banana slices. Certainly, the more the baby's food choices expand, the more interesting mealtime becomes.

Similarly, a new Christian would struggle if he or she tried to leap straight from salvation to debated, complicated doctrines. Perhaps some of those debates don't matter too much anyway. In the long run, what matters is distinguishing good from evil, and that comes from training oneself. For example, it may not occur to a new Christian that there are certain movies, books, music, and television shows that are poor choices for spiritual health. But the experienced, trained Christian would know we are to fill our minds with what is pure, admirable, and praiseworthy (Phil. 4:8).

The point of the verse is that, if we'll just move past those baby stages, there is so much more to learn. So much God can show us. But we must devote time to studying Scripture.

GROWING UP (HEB. 6:1–3)

The Greek word for *maturity* can also be translated as "perfection." Here, in the context of infants growing up, *maturity* may seem more suitable. I find the following thoughts from Gareth Cockerill to be a wonderful explanation of Hebrews 6:1: "This maturity or 'perfection' results neither from human achievement nor perfection of conduct. It is living in the full cleansing from sin, access to God, and victory over temptation provided by Christ."[1]

Who doesn't want to live like that? If we are willing to move past the basics and invest our time and energy in learning God's truth, then we can live victoriously in close communion with God! This is what Hebrews has been telling us. We have access to God. We have access to the power of Christ over sin. If only we will jump into our relationship with him with both feet, truly hearing what he has to say. We must pay attention to the words of God and not treat his message carelessly.

REFLECTION QUESTIONS

1. In what ways are you trying to further develop yourself as a believer?

2. What's your attention level on a Sunday morning? When the Word of God is being delivered, are you actively listening?

3. What is a realistic amount of time that a person can give to private Bible study and learning together with other Christians? Are you satisfied with the amount of time you're spending?

4. Be honest! How well do you know your Bible? Do you have a general idea of what most of the individual books of the Bible are about?

5. Would you be able to quickly find biblical support for the basic doctrines you believe? For example, if someone asked you where the Bible mentions what happens after we die, would you know where to look?

6. What does a mature Christian look like? Do you consider yourself a mature Christian? How does a person gain maturity?

PART 3

THE REAL
PROMISE

HEBREWS 6–8

12

LOSING ONE'S WAY VERSUS STAYING THE COURSE
HEBREWS 6:4–19

THOSE WHO FALL AWAY (HEB. 6:4–6)

If we have not found enough controversy yet in Hebrews, we've found it now. Here are people who cannot be "brought back to repentance" (v. 6). Many scholars find this passage terribly problematic and are unable to come to a conclusion as to its meaning. Yet even writers who believe that salvation cannot be lost or forfeited have noted that this is indeed a warning, not "a dissertation on the nature of grace, but . . . a warning in the strongest possible terms."[1] What is the point of a warning if there is no actual danger?

If the people described in the passage were never genuinely saved in the first place, then this passage is not about Christians losing salvation. John MacArthur says that within the group of people who originally received this epistle, there were non-Christians who were (only) "intellectually convinced." He believes that the point of this passage was to persuade them to make a heart commitment to Christ. "They believed that Jesus was the Messiah, the Christ, spoken of in the Jewish Scriptures . . . but they had not been willing to receive him personally as their Savior and Lord. Why? Perhaps . . . they believed in him, but they loved the approval of men more than the approval of God. . . . And so they are exhorted by the Holy Spirit to go all the way to saving faith."[2]

But let us look how these people are described. Verses 4–5 tell us they have:

- been enlightened,
- tasted the heavenly gift,
- shared in the Holy Spirit,
- tasted the goodness of the Word of God, and
- tasted the powers of the coming age.

MacArthur has a response for each of these things. For example, he says that they shared in the Holy Spirit only in the sense that "they simply were around when he was around."[3] They were never actually filled with the Spirit.

But it is difficult to look at this list and think that it describes unsaved people. In fact, for some scholars, there isn't any question: "All of the ways these people are described show that they have experienced the salvation brought by Christ."[4] In the Wesleyan tradition, we teach that it is possible for people who are saved to make a conscious decision to abandon their faith. We believe that people are always free to make their own decisions about a relationship with God.

To fully embrace a faith and then to consciously reject it is known as apostasy. And this Scripture passage certainly seems to teach that there is no coming back from it. Peter O'Brien says, "By not restoring those who commit apostasy, God allows their firm decision to stand. He does not force men and women against their obstinate resolve but allows them to terminate the relationship."[5]

RE-CRUCIFYING CHRIST (HEB. 6:6)

There was a popular Christian song in the 1990s that had these lyrics: "Does he still feel the nails every time I fail? Does he hear the crowd cry 'Crucify!' once again?"

Personally, I really don't think that Jesus relives the crucifixion every time a Christian misses the mark. But Hebrews tells us that apostasy does amount to re-crucifying Christ. To know him and to turn against him is to shame him and shout, "Crucify!" with the hypocrites at Jesus' trial.

CURSED AND BURNED (HEB. 6:7–8)

The illustration of the good land and the harsh land is easy to understand. Those who receive Christ and continue in him are fruitful and are blessed by God. Those who reject him are not.

It sounds as though the writer has backed down a bit when we read the phrase "in danger of being cursed" (v. 8)—almost as though the apostate has hope of escaping the curse. This, however, is a translation issue. The NRSV has the most accurate translation of this verse. It says that the barren land is "on the verge of being cursed." In other words, it's just a matter of time before the curse occurs. That may seem a bit unclear, but the statement about being burned is emphatic enough!

WHAT THE RECIPIENTS GOT RIGHT (HEB. 6:9–10)

Despite accusing the recipients of the letter of being spiritual infants, the author obviously had affection for them and faith in them. It is not expected that they would become apostates, but that they would commit themselves to the gospel. Their sincerity had been demonstrated by the love they've shown to God's people.

LAZY FAITH (HEB. 6:11–12)

The exhortation is for them not to become lazy. Consistency is called for—consistency until the end, whether that is the end of earthly life or the return of Christ. The words *diligence* and *patience*, describe what God wants from us. We are so blessed that God gives us his grace every time we err. Our High Priest understands our humanness. But knowing God gives grace freely is not an excuse for carelessness in our Christian walk. God expects lifelong dedication from us.

A number of years ago, a major clothing retailer had what they called their "Red Campaign." To visually show that you were in the fight against AIDS, you could buy a shirt or some other article of clothing that was red and had "RED" written across it. A fraction of the money you spent would help finance programs that supported AIDS victims in Africa. It struck me as rather strange to see people walking around like billboards, advertising the fact that they had done something good for the world. How heroic was this deed? If you bought one, you probably needed a shirt anyway. Besides, were you really personally committed to the fight against AIDS? Was the dime that this retailer sent on your behalf the only thing you contributed to the fight against the disease? If so, it really wasn't much of a commitment.

Sometimes people approach their faith like the Red Campaign. They make a small investment in their faith and expect God to say, "Ah, thank you so much! You've done your part." There's no diligence or perseverance. When there are demands that are uncomfortable, faith is put on the back burner. Maybe they stop their daily devotions because they got a new job that keeps them a bit busier. Maybe they disentangle themselves from church involvement because a new boyfriend or girlfriend persuades them to do other things. First they become inattentive to the things of God, then they find themselves drifting (2:1).

A lack of diligence is a dangerous thing. Faith and patience, however, will bring about "what has been promised" (6:12) — which we'll learn about in the next portion of Hebrews 6.

REFLECTION QUESTIONS

1. Above, I've stated that those of us in the Wesleyan tradition believe that people are always free to make their own decisions about a relationship with God. Do you agree that the choice is always ours? If so, do you see that as a negative or a positive? If you don't agree, what is your understanding of God's love through control?

2. Many of us have known friends and family members who have strayed from God and then returned to faith. It

may even be your own story. How are people with that sort of testimony different from the apostates described in Hebrews? When and how would a warning like this be useful in a modern church setting, if at all?

3. Apostates completely turn their backs on the salvation God gave them. Why would you never do this?

4. It certainly seems as though the door is closed for those who become apostates. Does this mean that God is unloving?

5. Do you think we Christians are in danger of losing our position in Christ on a daily basis, winding up cursed and burned, or is there greater security than that? How do you know you are secure in him?

13

GOD'S PROMISE
HEBREWS 6:13-20

BANK ON THIS (HEB. 6:13-18)

After talking about the dangers of losing faith, we come to the joy of resting in God's promise. Those who are faithful and patient need not fear. The most important message of the end of Hebrews 6 is that God's character is unchangeable. He is consistent; therefore, we can bank upon his promises.

To emphasize that his promise was reliable, God swore an oath on his own name. This oath was made to Abraham, but, as our writer pointed out, it was made so that the "heirs of what was promised" (v. 17) would know God's nature is enduring. The heirs are not the physical descendants of Abraham. They are his spiritual descendants—that is to say, us. "At one level, God promised Abraham descendants who would inherit the earthly Promised Land. However, the promise is truly fulfilled in Abraham's descendants by faith. They possess the heavenly homeland to which Abraham looked forward."[1]

Kevin Anderson says, "God's word of promise is bound to the steadiness of his own nature."[2] Because God's nature is unchangeable, his promises are eternal. In verse 17, God's purpose is described as having an "unchanging nature." The word translated as "unchanging," *ametathetos*, is a legal word.[3] It could also be translated as "irrevocable," which perhaps sounds even more definitive. There are, in fact, two unchangeable things (v. 18): the promise and the oath that confirms that promise. With these two rock-solid things, "God encourages them [and us] to go on in the life of faith."[4]

Even the most well-intended human promises are contingent at best. Imagine that a father promises to take his children to an amusement park on a specified day. Then he breaks his leg and cannot go. The promise was made with complete sincerity, but the father could not control the circumstances. Through no fault of his own, he could not keep his promise. This is never the case with God. He is omnipotent and therefore is not left powerless by circumstances. He guarantees his promises by his own name.

There has been an odd secularization of biblical promises in Western society of late. Some people do not claim a personal relationship with God, or they are the "drifters" we've read about in previous devotions, and yet they wish to claim God's promises for themselves. I have often heard people who aren't committed to Christ say, "God won't give me anything I can't handle." It would seem they are thinking of the promise in 1 Corinthians 10:13 that God won't let us be *tempted* (and by the way, God does not do the tempting—see James 1:13) beyond what we can endure. But this is a biblical promise made to the people of God. Those who ignore the uncomfortable parts of Scripture aren't really invited to make full application of the parts that put them at ease.

THE HOPE WE HAVE (HEB. 6:18–20)

The people to whom Hebrews was written, and the person who wrote it, had fled and grabbed hold of the hope Christ offers. From what were they fleeing? The old covenant? The threat of apostasy?

No one seems to have a certain answer. But the important thing is not what they ran *from*, but what they ran *to*. They ran to the hope that is found in Christ.

Our hope is described with three metaphors, all jumbled together in verses 19–20. First, it is described as an anchor. Christians of the twenty-first century understand the security of an anchor as well as the first Christians did. An anchor can be trusted every time.

But whereas anchors are dropped to provide security, the anchor in this metaphor has a different mission. "It enters the inner sanctuary behind the curtain" (v. 19; the inner sanctuary being the second metaphor). In the tabernacle of the Old Testament, a heavy curtain separated the main sanctuary from the holiest chamber. Behind that curtain was the presence of God. The anchor of our hope boldly moves behind that curtain.

Moving behind the curtain, we find that Jesus is already there. The third metaphor is that of the "forerunner, Jesus" (v. 20)—the fastest athlete, the one who easily won the race. Having reached the ultimate destination, the presence of the Father, he sat down, according to 1:3. He sat because he had completed all his priestly work. Today, he sits at God's right hand, because, being coequal in power and glory to God the Father, he has the right to sit.

REFLECTION QUESTIONS

1. Who are the inheritors of the promise?

2. What is the promise?

3. Do you feel secure in the reliability of God's promises? Why or why not?

4. Whose promises do you trust besides God's?

5. Has anyone ever deeply hurt you by breaking a promise?

6. What does God's promise-keeping record tell us about who he is? What does it tell us about who we are?

7. Do you remember fleeing from anything particular in your life as you ran toward Christ?

14

MELCHIZEDEK AND JESUS

HEBREWS 7:1–19

THE SIGNIFICANCE OF MELCHIZEDEK (HEB. 7:1–10)

In this passage, we encounter a biblical character (also mentioned in chs. 5–6) who doesn't really seem to be on the list of "Who's Who in the Old Testament." But when we read Hebrews, we can easily see that Melchizedek, who doesn't receive much prior biblical notice, was of great importance.

The author wanted to make sure the reader noticed four things. First, the meaning of Melchizedek's name. *Malak* is the Hebrew word for "king," and *tsedeq* (*ts* makes a *Z* sound, approximately) means "righteousness." The Hebrew language alters words slightly for a number of grammatical reasons. Here, when combining these two words, Melchizedek is the slightly altered result. "Salem" is akin to *shalom*, which most people will recognize as the Hebrew word for peace. Salem may also refer to Jerusalem, which would imply that Melchizedek was a king of Jerusalem. But that idea is suspect, since at that time the Hebrew city of Jerusalem would not have existed yet.[1] Whatever the case, his name and title mean King of Righteousness (or justice, which is actually a synonym for *righteousness*), King of Peace.

Second, he had no known genealogy. It is stated that he was without parents, but this simply means there is no written record of his family tree. It does not mean to imply that he was an orphan or that his parentage was dubious in some way. This mystery, this coming from nowhere, is meant to connote some sense of eternality.

Third, Melchizedek predated Levi, so his authority as a priest who deserved a tithe did not rest on ancestral privilege. In the future, Levites—the descendants of Levi who filled the priestly role—would regularly collect a tenth from the rest of the Israelites.

Fourth, in an odd twist, Levi, who wouldn't be born for generations, actually tithed to Melchizedek through Abraham, since Levi's DNA already resided in Abraham.

Melchizedek was a man of peace and justice (or righteousness). He did not stand on someone else's shoulders; he could not claim lofty lineage. We might say he was a self-made man. So highly regarded was he that even Abraham paid him tribute. We must not gloss over the importance of that; Abraham's homage is critical to understanding this passage. Abraham was the patriarch—the founder of the Hebrew nation and the adopted ancestor of even the Gentiles who come to believe in Christ. His tithe is a signifier of Melchizedek's exalted status.

With these things in mind, do you see similarities that would prompt the author to compare Jesus and Melchizedek?

CHANGE IN PRIESTHOOD, CHANGE IN LAW (HEB. 7:11–19)

People who had grown up in the Hebrew tradition were aware that the law of Moses and the Levitical priesthood that fulfilled its requirements were not perfect. Psalm 110:4 prophesied that a superior priest would come, and he would be in the order of Melchizedek: "The Lord has sworn and will not change his mind: 'You are a priest forever, in the order of Melchizedek.'" (It might be helpful to take the time to read all seven verses of Ps. 110.)

The Levitical priesthood had two inherent problems: It could not overcome human mortality, and its priests themselves were "prone to sin."[2] Having not been of the tribe of Levi, but of the tribe of Judah, "Jesus is completely unqualified for service in the Levitical priesthood. But he does not need to be, for he transcends it."[3]

The law and the priests who implement it cannot be separated. The old covenant, the old law, required Levitical priesthood. The prophecy of Psalm 110:4 meant that a new law, a new covenant, would be instituted. You could not have a new priest of a different tribe without a new law.

The old law involved faulty priests and an inability to overcome our sinful nature. The old law could not perfect anything. Our Perfect Priest, who inaugurated the new covenant, gives us the power to find victory over sin. We have a superior priest. We have a superior covenant. We have a reason to hope!

The last few words of Hebrews 7:19 are quite powerful. When the people of the Old Testament talked about drawing near to God, it was in reference to having purified themselves ritualistically. Such references were usually reserved for priests, who had to be ritually purified on a regular basis to conduct their sacrificial duty. But what a beautiful shift we have in this verse! Now we have a twofold promise that applies to all believers: We will draw near to him in the future in that we will actually be in his presence; and we have the right to draw near to him daily in prayer, and we may expect his involvement in the ordinary and troublesome concerns of our lives.

Try to imagine this shift. In the past, the Israelites were sinful people who had a faulty, earthly representative who entered the innermost chamber of the temple on their behalf.

Although he was imperfect, he ritually purified himself and made sacrifices on behalf of the people. The people could not enter the chamber. Under the new covenant, we have a Perfect Priest who offered *himself* as sacrifice. He was without blemish. And he forever destroyed barriers between God and us. He destroyed the veil that separated people from God's altar (Mark 15:38). He, as our High Priest, has given us license to approach God's throne with confidence (Heb. 4:14–16).

We have many stories of Old Testament heroes who had a relationship with God that was personal. Yet I suspect that any one of them would have envied what we have under the new covenant. How we mistreat our great privilege! Two things amaze me in particular: how infrequently we approach the throne of God, and how cavalier we are about our freedom to approach him. The people of the Old Testament would have longed for what we take for granted.

REFLECTION QUESTIONS

1. How does the author subtly use the comparison of Jesus and Melchizedek as an argument that Jesus is superior to Abraham?

2. How do you think your life, as a person of faith, would be different if you still lived under the old covenant?

3. Gareth Cockerill says that the new covenant "brings true cleansing from sin and enables people to actually come into the presence of and have fellowship with the living God."[4] Have you come into the presence of God and had fellowship with him? How do you prepare yourself for and achieve those encounters? If you don't feel you've enjoyed that kind of intimacy with God, can you find assurance in this passage that such a relationship is available to you?

4. What have you learned about the role of Jesus that perhaps you had not considered before?

15

THE PERMANENCY OF JESUS' PRIESTHOOD

HEBREWS 7:20–28

THE OATH AND THE GUARANTEE (HEB. 7:20–22)

The writer of Hebrews understood the power of an oath and called upon the idea to prove the reliability of God's plan. A guarantee or an oath seem like certainties to some but not all, depending on life circumstances.

In an earlier devotion, I mentioned that our family adopted two children. Just a couple of weeks before the one-year anniversary of their inclusion into our family, one of the children asked my husband, "When do we have to go to our new home?"

"What do you mean, 'our new home'?" he asked.

"You know, the next home."

Though we had spent a year assuring, promising, guaranteeing our children that we were their forever family, they could not process such an idea. Their biological mother had deemed it best to give them up for adoption, and then they spent eight months in a foster home—all by the time they were six and four years old. What reason had they to believe our guarantees of a forever home? Even if they tried, they simply could not wrap their minds around the concept.

Perhaps because so many of us have been let down by people's promises, we are reassured that Christ is the guarantor of the promise. The guarantor is the person who says, "I will make sure this comes to pass." If a young person wants to take out a loan, but his own credibility is not established, his parent may sign as a guarantor of the loan. That means that if the young person defaults, the parent will make the payments.

Jesus actually plays two roles here. Not only is he the guarantor, he is also the mediator of the covenant, which is to say that he puts it into effect. Of course, God is powerful enough to fulfill any promise. But, as the plan was designed, God the Father couldn't have fulfilled the oath of a new covenant without the participation (death and resurrection) of God the Son. So the Son is active as both mediator and guarantor. By putting the promise into action through his own sacrifice, he personally guarantees that the obligations of the covenant are met. As Cockerill says, "Jesus is a 'mediator' who *guarantees* what he mediates."[1]

So the promise—the new covenant—is guaranteed; it's ironclad. But what has God actually promised to us? We talked about this in the previous devotion a bit, but perhaps it is helpful to spell it out once more. The new covenant provides us with cleansing from sin and access to God— not in the imperfect way the old covenant did, but in the new, perfect way through the new, perfect sacrificial lamb and eternal priest, Jesus Christ. This is the first time the word *covenant* is used in the book of Hebrews. It bridges us to the next major portion of the book, "The Better Covenant."

THE PRIEST WHO MEDIATES FOREVER
(HEB. 7:23–25)

Jesus is the superior priest in so many ways, and one of those ways is that the post is permanent for him. Other priests were subject to death; Jesus lives eternally. For all who choose him, for all of time, he intercedes.

So much in life is unstable. Families change through birth and death and marriage and divorce. Even the climate of our earth, they say, is changing. I can hardly imagine how unsettling it would be if we had to worry that our High Priest, the One who served as go-between for us to the Father, could change.

In March 2013 Jorge Mario Bergoglio was named Pope Francis, the 266th pope of the Catholic Church. This humble man fascinates Protestants and Catholics alike. He certainly shook things up by throwing out the window what were typical parts of papal life. Pope Francis would live humbly, simply, denying the luxuries that other popes received as part of the position. While most of the world has greatly admired this, it certainly required mental reframing for both clergy and parishioners. A new pope brings a new style that requires adjustment on the parts of all those concerned. But imagine if we had to endure a shift in high priest. He stands before God on our behalf; what would it be like if the position were not stable?

Fortunately, we don't have to worry about that. Jesus lives forever, and his priesthood is permanent. Perhaps we are so used to the permanency of Christ's priesthood that we've never considered what a grace it is. The great lover of our souls, whose love is deep enough to prompt him to leave his throne and suffer for us, will forever stand as our representative before God the Father. This is no small thing.

THE MATCHLESS PRIEST (HEB. 7:26–28)

To sum up the chapter, the author stated that other priests were appointed in their human weakness, but the oath that came after the law of Moses brought a perfect priest. It is interesting that "the Son . . . has been made perfect forever" (v. 28). Wasn't Jesus *always* perfect? Why does it say he was *made* perfect? We visited this issue in devotion 6. Truly he was, is, and always will be morally perfect. His nature did not change. This verse refers to the fact that he was made perfect in his priestly function as a result of his sacrificial act. He was able to "exhaust the requisite of the office"[2] by virtue of his one great deed. The Son of God did not always fill the position of high priest; he was made the perfect priest forever when he completed his mission.

REFLECTION QUESTIONS

1. In your interactions with others, have you had a positive or negative experience with promises or oaths?

2. How do you think your experience affects the way you feel about an oath from God?

3. What are the differences between the law of Moses and the new covenant that came with the oath?

4. Jesus Christ stands alone as High Priest. None other has ever compared to him. How is he described in verse 26?

5. What words would you add to this list?

6. Throughout the first seven chapters of Hebrews, the author took great pains to show the supremacy of Christ

and his matchless perfection as our High Priest. How does this speak to you as a person (most likely a non-Jew) in the twenty-first century?

7. What verses in this first major division (chs. 1–7) of Hebrews have spoken most to you about who Christ is? What has spoken most to you about yourself?

16

REPLACING THE OBSOLETE

HEBREWS 8:1–13

OUR HIGH PRIEST SITS (HEB. 8:1)

The first couple verses of Hebrews 8, which express "the main point of what we are saying" (v. 1), serve as a bridge between "The Better Mediator" and "The Better Covenant." The fact that Christ surpasses any other priest was established in the previous three chapters of Hebrews. But the author would not move on without making sure the argument was abundantly clear. And so there is a conclusive statement in 8:1–2, which is really the apex of the argument. Our High Priest is perfect in his priesthood and has needed to offer only one sacrifice for all time (ch. 7). Therefore, he now sits "at the right hand of the throne of the Majesty in heaven" (8:1). He serves there eternally. "This point [that Christ sits, as no other priest has done in God's presence] has already been made in 1:3 of the Son, but is now repeated with direct application to the high-priest theme. This shows how carefully the writer has worked out this thesis, constantly throwing out hints which are gems in themselves but which sparkle with new meaning when seen again against a different background."[1]

COVENANT SHIFT (HEB. 8:2)

Although the second half of verse 2 flows naturally from the first half, it moves us into the new theme. It is here that the contrast begins between the man-made tabernacle and the "true tabernacle set up by the Lord" (v. 2). Christ and the other priests have been compared and contrasted. We know we have a superior mediator. Now, we turn to the other elements of the covenants.

THE SHADOWY TABERNACLE (HEB. 8:1–2, 5)

The tabernacle built in Exodus, after Moses made the covenant with God, was not a "false" tabernacle, in contrast to the "true" tabernacle. It was simply "an example or a mere shadow of the real one."[2] The true tabernacle is heavenly. It is where Christ has gone to sit beside the Father.

Remember that the tabernacle of Exodus was meant to represent the presence of God. Indeed, we can say that the *actual* presence of God was found there—but not in all fullness and only on occasion. It symbolized the heavenly dwelling of God where God's presence is full and constant.

Long after the Israelites ceased their nomadic lifestyle, Solomon built the temple. It was basically the same as the tabernacle—the difference being that it was a permanent structure, whereas the tabernacle was mobile. But there is another temple, another dwelling place of God, that comes in the space between the temple in Jerusalem and the heavenly tabernacle. It is within his people.

We have said that the true tabernacle is heavenly and Christ sits there. However, it might be seen as somewhat disingenuous to suggest that God the Father and God the Son have one physical location and remain there. It is hard to understand the metaphysics of a being that is not human. Even the dwelling of the Holy Spirit within believers is beyond the physical. We could not slice open a believer in Christ and see the Holy Spirit within. What is important to understand—more than any sort of idea of actual, physical location—is that the "true tabernacle" is the eternal reality of our access to God, which the Old Testament could only represent in a physical way. It "is a copy and shadow of what is in heaven" (v. 5) partly because it is confined by physical, substantive restraints.

THE SHADOWY MINISTRY (HEB. 8:3–6)

The high priest had one chief job: to offer sacrifice for sin. The writer says that "this one" (v. 3; Jesus) would also be required to bring a sacrifice. Although what that sacrifice was—his death—is not explicitly mentioned here. By comparison, the sacrifices the other high priests brought fell short.

In verse 4, the writer made a comment that almost seems absurd: Jesus would not qualify as an earthly priest. He wasn't of the right family—the Levite tribe—and he didn't offer the typical sacrifices. The point is that his priesthood exceeds earthly restraints. Earthly priests work in sanctuaries that are copies, says verse 5. Jesus' sanctuary is the real thing.

The ministry of Jesus is superior to that of the other priests, we read in verse 6. His tabernacle is eternal. His sacrifice was eternal. The high priests before him could offer nothing on par with that. Their ministry was but a shadow of his.

THE SHADOWY COVENANT GIVES WAY FOR THE NEW (HEB. 8:6–13)

We read that the new covenant that Christ brings us is "established on better promises" (v. 6). What are these promises? The promises we looked at in devotion 14, from Hebrews 7:19, are no doubt included; namely, that we have access to the presence of God now through prayer and access to him forever when we actually dwell where he dwells.

But there are more promises here. Verses 8–12 feature a lengthy quote from Jeremiah 31, where Jeremiah prophesied of the coming second covenant. You'll find five "better promises" here. The beautiful thing about these new promises is that they are so much more personal than what the old, shadowy covenant offered. The old law was written on tablets and memorized by the people. But now, God himself puts his law into his people's minds and writes it on their hearts. When he says he will be their (our) God and they (we) will be his people, he echoes what was taught throughout the Old Testament. But how much more intimate is that relationship now that God himself has inscribed his words into our hearts and minds? F. F. Bruce says, "'I will be your God' acquires fuller meaning with every further revelation of the character of God; 'you shall be my people' acquires deeper significance as the will of God for his people is more completely known.'"[3]

Hebrews 8:11 promises that all will know God. Remember that this is talking about all the *people of God*. It is not a declaration that all humankind will acknowledge him (as in Phil. 2). The covenant is with the "people of Israel" (Heb.

8:10). But whether or not Jeremiah understood it at the time of his writing, it is known throughout the New Testament that the people of God now includes any follower of God's Son, whether Jew or Gentile.

This verse does not imply that we should put an end to all Christian education because everyone automatically knows everything. Rather, the phrase "no longer will they teach their neighbor" (v. 11) is "a powerful rhetorical device"[4] meant to underscore the fact that all who believe will know God. Believers are not left in the cold until someone interprets or mediates for them. Our superior High Priest has seen to that, giving us access to the very throne of God. No believer is second tier.

Finally, we are promised forgiveness so thorough that most of us spend our lives struggling to comprehend it. Not only are our sins forgiven; the ultimate mind, the Origin of all thought and intelligence, will *forget* them. Not because he can't remember, but because he *wills* to forget. Most of us know what it is like to have our past mistakes or deliberate misdeeds thrown in our faces. Someone says, "Remember when you ____" And it hurts. No one has more right than God to bring up the past. Every sin is an offense against him, a rebellion. Yet while our parents, spouses, friends, or children may never wipe our record clean, our God does.

The old covenant was the foundation of the Hebrew faith. Through that covenant alone came restoration to God.

In short, it was everything. And now it was replaced. All of religion has been turned topsy-turvy!

In the legal system, the only person with the right to dissolve a covenant was the one who made it in the first place.[5] So, as appropriate, God alone could declare the old covenant obsolete.

REFLECTION QUESTIONS

1. Why did every other priest remain standing in the presence of God? Why did Christ sit?

2. Read 1 Corinthians 3:16. What is the current temple?

3. What are some of the ways in which Jesus is superior to any earthly priest? How is his service as a priest different from theirs?

4. Find and list the five promises in Hebrews 8:10–12. Hint: four begin with "I will" and one begins with "they will."

5. What do the five "better" promises of the new covenant tell us about the character of God?

6. What do the five promises mean in your life?

PART 4

THE BETTER
COVENANT

HEBREWS 9:1—10:18

17

THE EARTHLY TABERNACLE

HEBREWS 9:1–10

THE LAYOUT OF THE TABERNACLE (HEB. 9:1–5)

If the book of Hebrews was indeed written to Hebrew people, it is interesting that the writer took the time to describe the layout of the tabernacle, the model for the temple at the time. It is generally thought that the book was written while the temple was still standing, so even foreign Jews would understand the basic layout of the elemental objects so critical to the operation of their religion.

One might use this passage to argue for the idea that the book was written for non-Jews. However, since the entire book so thoroughly addresses all things Hebrew, the likelihood of a Jewish target audience still seems strongest.

The person who wrote Hebrews always underscored arguments with detail. Perhaps the review of the tabernacle was just a preparation for the upcoming comparison of the earthly tabernacle to the unearthly one, just as a history teacher would review World War I before proceeding to the Great Depression. Whatever the case, we can appreciate that it is helpful to us as twenty-first-century readers. Maybe it's simple: God had future, Gentile generations in mind as he inspired the writer to include this.

Let us then review the objects in the sanctuary that our writer mentioned.

WITHIN THE HOLY PLACE

THE LAMPSTAND

This stand, constructed of beaten gold, had a main stem with three branches coming out of both sides of the stem. It was a menorah. A lamp holder was located on the stem and each branch. The lamp holders were shaped like flowers and contained lights that burned all the time.

THE TABLE WITH ITS CONSECRATED BREAD

The table was made of acacia wood and had a gold overlay. Twelve loaves of unleavened bread lay on the table.[1] These loaves represented God's covenant with the twelve tribes of Israel. New loaves were placed on the table every Sabbath.

THE SECOND CURTAIN

The first curtain opened from the outer court into the Holy Place. The second curtain led to the Most Holy Place. It was made of blue, purple, and scarlet linen woven together with cherubim embroidered on it.

WITHIN THE MOST HOLY PLACE
(AKA THE HOLY OF HOLIES)

THE GOLDEN ALTAR OF INCENSE

This altar for incense burning invites a bit of controversy in the book of Hebrews, because according to the Old Testament it was located in the Holy Place, not the Most Holy Place. But for our purposes, it is not something we need to dwell on.

THE ARK OF THE COVENANT

The ark was about four-and-a-half feet long, two-and-a-half feet wide, and two-and-a-half feet deep. It was covered in gold and had a cherub at either end that faced down and inward. The cover was called the "atonement cover" or "mercy seat" and represented God's throne. The "glory" that dwelt on the cover indicated God's presence. The cherubim were the attendants to God as he resided there. When the high priest made sacrifice on the Day of Atonement (Yom Kippur), he sprinkled blood on the atonement cover.

INSIDE THE ARK

MOSES' STONE TABLETS FROM MOUNT SINAI

The ark held the physical copy of the law (the Ten Commandments) and God's original covenant with the Israelites.

THE GOLD JAR OF MANNA

This was a sample of the manna God provided for the Israelites in the desert.

AARON'S STAFF

When God chose Aaron and his tribe as his priests, he verified the choice by a miracle: Aaron's staff budded, blossomed, and produced almonds (Num. 17:8).

(Other Scripture verses indicate that these items were placed before, not within, the ark.)

THE WORK OF THE PRIESTS (HEB. 9:6–7)

Any priest could work in the Holy Place. The lamps had to be trimmed regularly, so the lights never stopped burning. Once a week, the bread was replaced.

The Most Holy Place was frighteningly sacred. Only the high priest could go there, and only on Yom Kippur (Day of Atonement). He offered a bull sacrifice for his own sins, and then a goat sacrifice for the sins of the people. Regarding this sacrifice, Kevin Anderson makes an interesting argument: "Hebrews rightly discerns atonement as limited to unintentional sins (see Lev. 4:1—5:19; Num. 15:22–29). Those who sinned defiantly were subject to the death penalty (Ex. 21:14; Num. 35:20–21, 30–31; Deut. 17:12) or its equivalent—exclusion from the people of God (Num. 15:30–31). Yom Kippur could not benefit them. Hebrews maintains the rigorist position that rebellious or high-handed sins are unpardonable (Heb. 6:4–8)."[2]

Though it is appropriate to distinguish between sins that are and are not intentional, I find two significant problems with Anderson's assertion. First, one must consider those in the Old Testament who knowingly committed sins but were forgiven, such as David. Second, while many (including myself) interpret Hebrews as saying that a loss of salvation is possible, it is a great leap to say that *any* sin that a person commits on purpose is, or has ever been, unforgivable. Surely that is not the point here.

Some Christians take sin very lightly. They feel they can be forgiven, so it isn't a big deal if they commit a few infractions here and there. In fact, quite a few Christian songs and books seem to boast about the fact that it is OK to keep on sinning—God doesn't expect perfection, they say. Having come this far in the study of Hebrews, what do you think the writer of Hebrews would say to a Christian who felt this way?

THE SHADOW THE CURTAIN CAST (HEB. 9:8–10)

Anderson points out that it was typical for the author of Hebrews to give the Holy Spirit credit for scriptural revelation. The Holy Spirit revealed that the tabernacle required rules and physical structures to keep the people, and the regular priests, in their place. Access to God knew its limits. God was a shadowy figure behind the curtain. As long as the first room of the tabernacle—the Holy Place—existed, the restrictions stood. It was a physical illustration of a spiritual barrier. F. F. Bruce puts it bluntly: "Throughout the age of the old covenant there was no direct access to God."[3]

Having discussed blood sacrifice already, our writer next referred to the responsibilities of the ordinary worshiper under the old covenant. All the people were to live by a specific diet God had delineated and be diligent about ceremonial washings. But these procedures were only external, physical. With that in mind, we arrive at a major point.

"Now we see what our author wishes to teach his readers. The really effective barrier . . . free access to God is an inward and not a material one; it exists in the conscience. It is only when the conscience is purified that one is set free to approach God without reservation and offer him acceptable service and worship."[4]

REFLECTION QUESTIONS

1. Why were each of the items in the ark important enough to be preserved? What did these items represent?

2. How do these priestly duties strike you, in light of the duties of a modern pastor/officer/church staff member?

3. Why did God have his priests carry out these tasks, rather than a servant or helper?

4. The functions of the tabernacle were set up to erase human sin. Based on what you see in this chapter, what is God's attitude toward sin?

5. What is your attitude toward your own sin?

18

THE BLOOD OF CHRIST

HEBREWS 9:11–14

WHEN CHRIST CAME (HEB. 9:11–12)

The book of Hebrews doesn't focus on Christ's life and role on earth. The author was more concerned with what happened when the messianic work was done, as we have seen throughout our devotions. In verse 11, the author did not refer to Christ's incarnation on earth when he wrote, "When Christ came." This is another instance that refers to Christ as returning to the Father and sitting at his right hand. It was then that Christ came as High Priest. His priesthood is not of earth and has none of the elements of earthly priesthood. It began after his sojourn as a human on our planet.

He is High Priest of "the good things that are now already here" (v. 11). Earthly priesthood dealt with lamps, bread, and animal sacrifice. People concerned themselves with ceremonial washings and proper dietary habits. These were the temporal, external things that were in effect "until the time of the new order" (v. 10). The contrast of the new order, which brings the "good things," is seen in the next few verses. These good things are the better covenant. Remember the five promises in 8:10–12 (devotion 16)? Perhaps those serve as a summary of the "good things."

MORE PERFECT TABERNACLE (HEB. 9:11–12)

Understand that the tabernacle has always represented the presence of God. The ancient Israelites had to build a hand-made tabernacle to show God's presence. My husband once said that in some ways the early Israelites were fortunate. They could see God's presence—in a sense—with their very eyes. I wouldn't trade the new covenant for the old (and neither would my husband!), but I must agree that it would be nice to have a physical reminder of God's presence, right within one's sightline, every day. But the work of the Superior Priest is not done in a handmade tent. It is in a realm beyond. He is in the perfect, complete presence of God the Father.

If I could come to wherever you are right now and underline four words in your Bible, they would be these: *once*, *all*, *own*, and *eternal* (v. 12). The author of Hebrews attempted to drive these points home since chapter 1. The sacrifice of Christ was required only *once* to atone for *all* humankind, because it was Christ's *own* perfect blood, and that perfection made his work *eternal*. He is the Ultimate Priest.

BLOOD SACRIFICE (HEB. 9:13–14)

We have read much about the blood sacrifices. In verse 13, there is also reference to the use of the ashes of a heifer to purify someone who is ceremonially unclean. This recalls an event that took place in Numbers 19:9–13. What matters, of course, is that these procedures only purified people externally.

I have often wondered why blood sacrifice is necessary. You may have wondered about that, too. After all, God made the rules. Couldn't he have decided that if we were just really, really sorry our sins would be erased? Or if that's too easy, couldn't he have designed another plan? Maybe he could have required a pilgrimage to atone for our sins?

I don't know God's reasoning, but there are a couple thoughts that come to mind. In 1 Chronicles 21, David wanted to make an altar and offer a sacrifice to the Lord. One of his loyal subjects offered to provide the oxen for the sacrifice, at no charge to King David. The powerful response David gave has rung through the centuries: "I insist on paying the full price. I will not take for the LORD what is yours, or sacrifice a burnt offering that costs me nothing" (1 Chron. 21:24). In the days of animal sacrifice, the best—least blemished—animals were offered to the Lord. Surely this was at great expense to many people. Even to King David it was not "nothing." The blood sacrifice involves loss. Penitence is more potent if loss is involved.

The requirement of blood sacrifice would ultimately lead to an unimaginable demonstration of God's love. I can't pretend to know the reasoning of God in the plan of salvation, but could this possibly have had something to do with it? Did he set up a system that would eventually lead to Christ's sacrifice, in order that such a gesture would endear him to us?

The author compares the blood of mere animals to what Peter O'Brien calls "the incalculable value of [Christ's] sacrifice."[1] The old sacrifices cleaned people "so that they are outwardly clean" (Heb. 9:13). But the blood of Christ can "cleanse our consciences from acts that lead to death" (v. 14). In the previous devotion, we noted the trouble underscored in 9:9—that the conscience was not cleared by the old covenant. The writer completed his point now, celebrating the cleansing of the conscience by Jesus' blood. Our idea of "conscience" may be slightly different from that of the writer of Hebrews. William Lane explains, "In

Hebrews the term has deeply religious overtones; the 'conscience' is directed toward God and embraces the whole person in his relation to God."[2]

When I think of a clean conscience, I think of not *feeling* guilty. When Hebrews speaks of a clean conscience, it means not *being* guilty. But really, the blood of Christ is meant to deal with both those issues, isn't it?

SPECIAL BONUS (HEB. 9:14)

Early on in this book, I expressed a wish that God had made the doctrine of the Trinity unmistakable in Scripture. I wish the word *Trinity* could actually be found—it would make things simpler for us! But here is a lovely bonus in Hebrews. The writer lays the idea of the Trinity before us by mentioning all persons of the Godhead in one breath. All three expressions of the Godhead are working together, toward one end: a redemption that leads us back into fellowship with God. "How much more, then, will the blood of Christ, who through the eternal Spirit offered himself unblemished to God, cleanse our consciences from acts that lead to death, so that we may serve the living God!" (v. 14).

I appreciate the status of the Holy Spirit in this verse. Christ did not offer himself in his own strength alone. He did so "through the eternal Spirit." Lane says, "'Through the eternal Spirit' implies that [Christ] had been divinely empowered and sustained in his office.'"[3] We see how key the role of the Spirit has been in our salvation.

REFLECTION QUESTIONS

1. Look at Hebrews 9:12. How did the priests enter into the presence of God?

2. How did Jesus enter the perfect Most Holy Place?

3. What would you suggest as a possible reason that God has required blood sacrifice?

4. If our consciences have been cleansed, why do we sometimes feel guilty for past sin?

5. Is it possible that we insult the sacrifice of Christ by hanging on to the guilt he died to erase?

6. How do you think the writer of Hebrews would define *conscience*?

7. Traditionally the church has used the phrase "cleansed our hearts from sin." What do you think might be a better way to describe the cleansing that has taken place?

8. In what way do you think the Holy Spirit empowered Christ to make his sacrifice? Why would Jesus Christ, Son of God, need to be empowered?

9. How does the Holy Spirit empower you to live a sacrificial life?

19

THE MEDIATOR

HEBREWS 9:15–22

THE ETERNAL INHERITANCE (HEB. 9:15)

For a number of chapters, we read the description of Christ as High Priest. In Hebrews 8, he was referred to as mediator, and here we find that designation again. Certainly it had been implied all throughout the book. But here the author made the statement that Christ is mediator of the new covenant, and gave the reason why: so those who are called will receive their eternal inheritance.

In the book of Hebrews, the word *eternal* seems to imply a sense of completeness as well as a sense of unending. It is full, it is the best, nothing could ever add to it, and so it is eternal. The writer used the word *eternal* on several occasions. It is key when comparing the benefits of the old covenant with the benefits of the new. In 5:9, the great High Priest offers "eternal salvation"; in 9:12, "eternal redemption." "Eternal Spirit" is used in reference to the Holy Spirit in 9:14. Later we will read about the "eternal covenant" itself. But here we have the promise of "eternal inheritance." Donald Guthrie writes, "The idea of inheritance was central in the old covenant but it did not rise above the earthly level. Here it is eternal, hence clearly superior. This is the real fulfillment of the promise."[1]

This eternal inheritance — our redemption and access to God — is promised to "those who are called" (v. 15). A good many biblical Christians believe that certain persons are elected by God to be saved, while other persons are not. Several verses describing believers as the "called" are used in support of that view. An alternate view is that everyone is called, but not everyone responds. This is not a point worth belaboring here. Clearly, the point in this passage is that *this* inheritance is for *these* people — the saved. The author is not making a case for or against the doctrine of election.

FREEDOM IN FORGIVENESS (HEB. 9:15)

The sacrifices of the Old Testament did the job they were intended to do: bring forgiveness. But they could not completely remove sins committed as though they never happened. Hence, Christ came to "set them free from the sins committed under the first covenant" (v. 15). The point is not that sins that were committed in the time period before the new covenant are now retroactively forgiven (though that makes an interesting discussion). The author simply wants to stress that what the old system couldn't erase, the new system can.

Most human relationships dwell in an Old Testament reality. We may forgive each other, but we never quite clear the record. An adult child doesn't easily forget the mistakes her parents made while raising her. A husband finds himself unable to fully acquit his wife of her affair. Friends who once parted ways may be able to regain only a fragile friendship. First Corinthians 13 says love keeps no record of wrongs. But how does one do that? How is it possible to forget how others have hurt us?

We can only love like that because Christ has loved us, and we are only enabled through the power of the Holy Spirit. However, while so many of us enjoy the full grace of God through the blood of Jesus Christ, we don't think about extending that kind of grace to others. We may forgive, but we refuse to forget. In so doing, we receive the new covenant for ourselves but neglect to appropriate it in our relationships. We live with one foot in each covenant. Surely Christ did not die for such incompleteness. Surely he expects us to extend to others the grace he lavished on us.

Some say they will forgive so they themselves can be truly free. It is common knowledge that stewing in bitterness hurts the victim even more than the perpetrator (if it hurts the perpetrator at all!). Yet the idea of forgiving for one's own sake, which has taken firm root in the Christian world, is troubling. When Christ offered himself as the perfect sacrifice, was his first intent his own happiness? Did the Father send the Son for some sense of personal relief? Certainly not! John 3:16 gives us the reason for the blood sacrifice: "For God so loved the world."

It is true that forgiving those who have offended us will help us heal our own hearts. But if we are to model ourselves after Christ, we are to forgive for the sake of the offender first and foremost. Think of the mercy shown the apostle Paul: "Even though I was once a blasphemer and a persecutor and a violent man, I was shown mercy because I acted in ignorance and unbelief. The grace of our Lord was poured out on me abundantly, along with the faith and love that are in Christ Jesus" (1 Tim. 1:13–14).

Isn't it time that we apply new covenant principles in our human relationships? Is there a person who needs your complete forgiveness and forgetfulness, just as Christ has granted to you? In the strength of the Holy Spirit, are you willing to erase the record against that person?

REQUISITE MET (HEB. 9:16–22)

In Hebrews 9:16, the author made a temporary shift: he referred to a "will" as opposed to the covenant—which is nice rhetorical support for the claim in verse 15 that the people who are called receive an "inheritance."

The author pointed out that a will is ineffective unless the testator is actually dead. Kevin Anderson states that "the central point in the discussion is that Christ has died."[2] The will could not have activated had Christ merely fainted, as some groups have claimed throughout history. By now, we see the picture. Blood. Death. These things are essential requisites for salvation. "Without the shedding of blood there is no forgiveness" (v. 22).

The inauguration of the old covenant (Ex. 24), at least to the modern mind, borders on gory. Perhaps the burning bull meat was a pleasant smell, not unlike the aroma that hits you when you walk into a steak restaurant or burger joint. But Moses took the blood of the bulls and splashed it on the altar and then on the people. Can you imagine having animal blood sprinkled over you as part of a spiritual ritual? While it must have been quite unpleasant, I guess nobody could have missed the point. Today, it is over two thousand years since the spilled blood of our Savior was witnessed at Calvary. And maybe sometimes we do miss the point. We talk and sing about the blood of Christ so much that we aren't necessarily moved by it. Besides that, we weren't there. We didn't see it, smell it, or feel it splash out at us, as perhaps Mary or John did as they wept at the cross.

It is human nature to take for granted what you've always known. My kids are absolutely nonchalant over the fact that they can reach any friend or relative at any time. They have social media, Skype, and best of all, the ever-portable cell phone. If you're as old as I am, you remember the hassle of arranging to meet a friend for lunch only to sit waiting if she didn't show up. Did she go to the wrong restaurant? Did her car break down? Did she actually say Thursday when you thought she said Tuesday? Was she just late? How long should you wait? Today, a simple call or text answers all our questions.

Similarly, the people of the Old Testament endured the hassles of their era, and probably couldn't fully envision the ease and grace of life after the Messiah. We can't fully understand the blessed situation we find ourselves in. But it is a good idea to try.

REFLECTION QUESTIONS

1. How do we benefit from our eternal inheritance now? How will we benefit from it into eternity?

2. In what ways do we take the eternal inheritance and the blood of Christ for granted?

3. Draw a picture of the crucifixion of Christ, or write a poem about it. (Talent is not necessary!) As you do so, really reflect on what Christ suffered for us.

20

THE BLOOD OF CHRIST, CONTINUED
HEBREWS 9:23–28

BLOOD AND HEAVENLY THINGS (HEB. 9:23–24)

In devotion 18, we compared the blood of animals to the blood of Christ. The discussion continues here at the end of Hebrews 9. The blood of animal sacrifices was sufficient to cleanse the furniture of the tabernacle. And, as we have seen, it could alleviate the immediate guilt of the people but could not completely dispense with their sin. The "heavenly things"—those *not* within "a sanctuary made with human hands" (v. 24)—needed the eternal sacrifice.

Why would "heavenly things" need any cleansing at all? F. F. Bruce says, "Our author has provided the answer in the context. What needed to be cleansed was the defiled conscience of men and women; this is a cleansing which belongs to the spiritual sphere."[1]

Whereas the earthly tabernacle had actual religious relics, it is likely that there is no furniture per se in the heavenly tabernacle, so the author is not being literal when he talks about "heavenly things" or "copies of the heavenly things" (v. 23). The point is that there is a higher order, and the higher order deals directly with the souls of human beings. Souls—"consciences"—need more than animal blood to purify them.

THE CULMINATION OF THE AGES (HEB. 9:25–26)

We are reminded again of the completeness of Christ's sacrifice. Once and only once was this necessary. In previous devotions, we have noted that Christ was able to sit down in the presence of God as a result of the thoroughness of his saving work. Imagine if Christ had to die annually (like Yom Kippur's yearly sacrifice) to pay the price for our sin! It would mean that Christ was not enough. It would cast doubt on his deity. But the truth is, he is utterly sufficient. He is an equal person in the Trinity; he is God. How could any offering of his not be complete?

Christ's sacrifice was made "at the culmination of the ages" (v. 26). The phrase has also been translated as "end of the ages," "consummation of the ages," or "the climax of history." While *end* or *culmination* seems to imply that

149

this moment was the end of the history of Earth, we certainly know that wasn't true. The history of the world peaked because sin was conquered at that moment. On that afternoon, the record was cleared for anyone throughout history who would choose to appropriate that blood. That incomparable deed was in itself the climax of the human story and the climax of God's plan to restore humankind to himself.

THE END OF SIN? (HEB. 9:26)

This verse says that Christ died to "do away with sin." But people are still sinning; even Christians are still sinning. So what does "do away with sin" mean?

We read in verse 15 that Christ's death set people free from sin. While people still continue to commit sin, some very important things have happened:

- Sin no longer condemns those who believe; death has lost its sting.
- God views us through the blood of Christ. Though he is aware of our struggles, he regards us as completed and perfected, not as sinners.
- We are never powerless against sin. Every time we sin it is because we choose to do so.

Although sin still exists in this world, according to the Wesleyan tradition, through the power of the Holy Spirit, we are able to live a life without willful sin. If a person is living without willful (intentional) sin, some infractions against God and people may still occur out of ignorance, because we are only human. But it is possible to be so submissive to God and so full of his love that we don't opt for sin any longer. "To insist that believers are necessarily sinful, or that they continue to be prone to personal sin, is to limit the power of the atonement to bring about a thorough change of character and a comprehensive victory over sin."[2]

Do not be fooled. You aren't powerless against sin. Sin is powerless against the Spirit in you.

ONE SACRIFICE, MANY BENEFICIARIES (HEB. 9:27–28)

As we read that Christ died once just as people die only once, we are reminded of the humanity of Christ, which he took on voluntarily (see Phil. 2). It is good to consider that point while reading this passage, because becoming human was part of the sacrifice of Christ. When he set aside his glory and power, he did it for "the sins of many" (Heb. 9:28). It was not only for the inconsequential sins of the most deserving people. In fact, "many" does not mean a select group.

Rather, the word is used to contrast with the *one* sacrifice. One giver, many recipients.

Indeed, if Osama bin Laden pleaded the blood of Jesus in his last moments, then it was applied to him. You see, "God so loved *the world* that he gave his one and only Son. . . . *Whoever* believes in him is not condemned" (John 3:16, 18, emphasis added). If we fully understood that God loves everyone equally, if we meditated on that and made it part of our daily consciousness, we'd stop gossiping, competing, envying, and stereotyping. If God loves you and me, why do we defame or resent those he loves as much as us?

Think about the person you find most difficult to appreciate. If you dare, write that person's name here: _____. Perhaps that person may even be a prominent politician or other noted person whom you don't know personally. The fact that you don't actually know that person doesn't mean it is OK with God for you to disdain him or her. Consider what qualities God sees in that person that are pleasing to him.

Whenever you see or think of that person, view him or her through the eyes of God as best you can. Remember that the perfect, eternal sacrifice of Christ's blood was made on behalf of that person, too—whether or not that person has chosen to receive it. (And by the way, you and I are not the judges of whether or not that person has received it. That's God's job!)

HE COMES, BRINGING SALVATION (HEB. 9:28)

Christ has promised to return, and we await that return. This verse says he will "bring salvation to those who are waiting for him." Salvation from sin has already been completed. Those who are waiting are those who have received it. But the salvation we are still waiting for is the fulfillment of all that has been promised to us.

"All the blessings which he won for his people at his first appearing will be theirs to enjoy in perpetual fullness at his second appearing. Therefore, let them not grow faint and weary but persevere in patience and faith."[3]

REFLECTION QUESTIONS

1. Describe the moment you decided that you wanted the sacrifice of Christ applied to your sin.

2. Look up Romans 8:1–4. What truths here are echoed in Hebrews?

3. Read Romans 3:21–24 and 4:5–8. What does your faith do for you?

4. Read Titus 2:11–12. What worldly passions do you need to forsake?

5. Do you agree that it is possible to live a life in which you constantly have victory over sin? Why or why not?

21

THE PERFECT SACRIFICE, THE PERFECT WORSHIPER

HEBREWS 10:1–18

OUR TEACHER PROVIDES A REVIEW (HEB. 10:1–10)

You will note that this passage reviews a few of the major points our writer had hit on before. In fact, we've read some of these truths multiple times. A teacher who takes pride in tripping up his students doesn't spend much time reviewing. Then he tests his students on things they didn't even realize were important. But when a teacher's primary objective is for his students to really learn the material, he emphasizes the critical points repeatedly. He puts them on the review sheet. When he tests on those points, nobody is caught off guard.

Our writer was a teacher of the highest caliber. As such, he reiterated his main points. Sometimes he did so because he was building upon a previous argument, and other times it was just because he didn't want anyone to miss his main point. Now, the second major chunk of Hebrews is coming to a close. The first two divisions of Hebrews were theological, but the third section is practical. So, for the most part, the theological assertion of the book is being wrapped up. It comes as no real surprise, then, that our extremely thorough author would underscore his salient points one last time.

Let's look first at what those major review statements are in this passage.

1. "The law is only a shadow of the good things that are coming—not the realities themselves" (v. 1).
2. "It is impossible for the blood of bulls and goats to take away sins" (v. 4).
3. "We have been made holy through the sacrifice of the body of Jesus Christ once for all" (v. 10). (In this context, *holy* means washed of sin, acceptable to God.)
4. "When this priest had offered for all time one sacrifice for sins, he sat down at the right hand of God" (v. 12)

Notice how one statement leads logically to the next. Salvation under both covenants is distilled into a four well-crafted, sequential sentences.

BEING MADE PERFECT (HEB. 10:1–4)

When found in the Bible, the word *perfect* makes people nervous. Often there are other ways to translate the word, and a person's theological preferences may show based on which translation they prefer. In this case, however, every major translation uses the word *perfect*. Gareth Cockerill helps us understand how the word is being used. "By 'made perfect,' he means that God's people are cleansed from sin within, given a new heart that knows and obeys God's law, and thus enabled by God to live in obedience. Those old repeated sacrifices could never truly help people forward. Their repetition proves they could not."[1]

The expression "felt guilty" may also need some explanation. "It might be more accurate to say that they would no longer have had any 'consciousness' (NKJV; NASB; NRSV) . . . of sin. More than guilt is involved. [If animal sacrifice had been sufficient,] they would have been free from the guilt *and* the pollution and power of sin. God's grace would have freed them from sin to live for God, victorious over temptation."[2]

Cockerill teases out the notion of freedom from the stronghold of sin. Had the blood sacrifices been complete—as would be the coming sacrifice of Christ—guilt would be erased, the sins committed would be forgiven, and sin would have no control over the life of the worshiper. But not every commentator reads as much into this remark as Cockerill does. William Lane, for example, explains that when the Day of Atonement came, the Israelites had a "burdened, smitten heart" and "as long as [their] sense of sin and transgression . . . remained, there could be no effective service of God." In his understanding, what the Israelites lacked was the "decisive cleansing of the conscience."[3] He says nothing about being liberated from sin's grip on one's life.

What Cockerill is saying may not be the major thrust of this passage. But since he raised the notion, let us consider it for a moment. The question is: Does the ultimate blood sacrifice cleanse from guilt and sin, or does it go so far as to completely incapacitate sin in the life of the worshiper?

We can look at our fellow Christians and even ourselves and realize that most Christians keep on sinning, hopefully not as vigorously as before their salvation; but still, most commit conscious, deliberate sins. White lies. Gossip. Insults. Sneers. And of course, sometimes the big stuff: adultery, theft, and so on. What is being considered here is whether or not a Christian will inevitably sin. Should we resign ourselves to the fact that we are only human and we will continue to commit willful sin?

If we don't grasp the fact that it is possible for us to live without purposefully sinning, then we have not fully grasped the difference between animal sacrifice and the blood of

Christ. If we convince ourselves that sin is inevitable, we deny that we are empowered to live beyond the guilt of sin and we shortchange the power of the blood. The finality of the blood of Christ means we don't have to willfully sin. Christ has put an end to the power of sin. If it were not so, wouldn't the sacrifice need repeating?

THE PROPHECY IN PLAY (HEB. 10:5–10)

The writer of Hebrews helped us to understand that Psalm 40:6–8 is a prophecy concerning Jesus. The prepared body was his, and he subjected himself to the will of the Father by offering that body up. The writer of Hebrews gave a small commentary on the psalm in verses 8–9, noting that the offerings that didn't please God were what the law had required, but that the initial will of God (the law and the animal sacrifice) was set aside to fulfill God's ultimate will.

Many years ago, I taught high school choir. When I heard the choir sing on our very first day, it was awful. But we worked and worked and worked. We labored over particular phrases of our music every day. We reviewed each note, each dynamic, each lyric. By the time our fall concert arrived, I was proud. All but one person sang in the written key, most of the harmony could be heard, and the choir members sang with confidence. We took the weekend off, but come Monday, it was time to begin working hard on the winter concert.

I have participated in vocal groups that were very different from that high school choir. A few groups I've been in had such experienced singers that one good rehearsal was all it took, and the music was performance ready. The caliber of the singers was far higher than that of my eager but inexperienced high schoolers.

Sacrifice under the law was something like music with the high school choir. The intention was noble, and they gave the very best they had to offer. But through no fault of their own, they couldn't possibly measure up to more experienced singers. The law did all it could to produce forgiveness. But, like my singers, it was limited. As my singers had to work and work to get good—but not superb—results, so the priests of the old covenant had to sacrifice and sacrifice to make incomplete amends.

There was a shortfall. But Christ offered himself up to the will of God, and through his enormous sacrifice, he satisfied every requirement. The insufficient was replaced by the wholly sufficient. We are the beneficiaries.

"The sanctification which his people receive in consequence [of Christ's sacrifice] is their inward cleansing from sin and their being made fit for the presence of God."[4] This is a qualifying holiness. The blood of Christ qualifies us to draw near to God.

COMPLETING THE VICTORY (HEB. 10:11–13)

The saving work of Christ is done, but one last step remains for his victory to be complete: "He waits for his enemies to be made his footstool" (v. 13). This is not in question. Just as every other prophecy about Christ has been fulfilled, so this one will be fulfilled. Jesus' enemies aren't listed, but we can assume they include the Devil and his minions, those who reject the blood that was shed for their salvation, and the apostates who first accepted Christ but unforgivably turned from him forever. The day will come when these enemies will be completely subjugated. And they will be unable to affect the people of God ever again.

OUR PERFECTION (HEB. 10:14–18)

We were "made perfect" when we received the blood that qualified us to stand before God. We are "being made holy" in that God continues to refine us and we must continue to submit ourselves to his ongoing work. We will soon read about the discipline and consistency required by God, which is the ongoing work. But the major emphasis in verse 14 is on what I have referred to as "qualifying holiness." That is to say, it is the status conferred upon us as soon as we receive the blood of Christ. It is what makes us saints in God's eyes instead of sinners.

If the animal sacrifices had been sufficient, they would have cured the people of the disease of sin, giving them hearts that understood God's laws. They would have given the people the ability to live correctly, and the sacrifices would not have needed repeating. But, as the Holy Spirit promised us through Jeremiah in Jeremiah 31:33 (see also Heb. 10:16), under his new covenant the Lord has indeed put his laws in the hearts and minds of believers, purifying their consciences. He has defeated sin permanently and made us his own.

God has forgotten our "sins and lawless acts" (v. 17). We would do well to remember that because God refuses to remember our past misdeeds, they are completely and utterly irrelevant. Any guilt over forgiven sin that haunts us is not from the Lord. It is from the Enemy. What makes us think that we have the right to beat ourselves up over what Christ's blood has already washed away? Are you or I a higher judge than God?

Is there an issue of past sin in your life that the Enemy continues to whisper in your ear, causing you guilt? Ask the Holy Spirit to help you ignore the Devil's taunts and release that guilt forever.

REFLECTION QUESTIONS

1. Do you agree that willful sin is not inevitable for believers? How would you defend your position?

2. Is it possible that we shortchange the power of Christ's blood if we think we can't live without sinning? Why or why not?

3. There is a difference between sin that is intentional, or willful, and sin that is committed in ignorance. Can you think of examples of each?

4. I've used the term "qualifying holiness." What is it, and why is it crucial?

5. The theological argument of Hebrews is now basically concluded. Have you gained any new insights about the nature of Christ in these chapters? What has stood out to you about the differences between the old covenant and the new?

PART 5

THE PRACTICAL
IMPLICATIONS

HEBREWS 10:19—11:31

22

PERSEVERE IN THE FAITH

HEBREWS 10:19–25

THE THINGS THAT GIVE US ACCESS (HEB. 10:19–22)

As Hebrews progresses toward words of exhortation, we have the opportunity to quickly review all we have learned since the end of Hebrews 4. We approach the throne because of the blood of Jesus, we have a great High Priest, and our consciences are cleansed.

Throughout Hebrews, the author wrote surprisingly little about the curtain that divided the main room of the tabernacle and temple from the Most Holy Place. The tabernacle structure was described well in chapter 9, and we understand how the curtain symbolized the inaccessibility of God. In 6:19, we read that Jesus has gone through the curtain on our behalf. But until now, nothing else has been said about the curtain.

Mark's gospel tells us this: "With a loud cry, Jesus breathed his last. The curtain of the temple was torn in two from top to bottom" (15:37–38). Mark spoke of a literal curtain, but here the writer of Hebrews used figurative language. A complication accompanies our interpreting this figurative use of the curtain in Hebrews 10:20: "By a new and living way opened for us through the curtain, that is, his body." We are inclined to think that his body is the "new and living way" that opened the curtain. But many scholars agree that in this verse Jesus' body is the curtain. "So the enigmatic expression through the curtain, that is, *through* his body is a succinct way of saying that access to God's presence has been achieved through Christ's bodily death."[1] Either way you look at it, the point is that entrance to the presence of God has become possible.

Of course, it is of no consequence to us that the curtain is gone unless we have had our "guilty conscience" cleansed (v. 22). Again we bump up against this troubling word, *conscience*. It is a difficult word because it doesn't seem to mean as much to us as it did to the writer of Hebrews. Gareth Cockerill says, "Literally translated, the phrase 'guilty conscience' is 'evil conscience' (NASB). Christ cleanses our inner selves from the guilt and power of sin. He gives us an inclination to obey God."[2] It needs to be stressed again that it isn't just a matter of not feeling guilty anymore. By cleansing our conscience, Christ gives us the power to choose not to sin.

Listed with these other things that give us accessibility to God is "having our bodies washed with pure water" (v. 22). William Lane says, "The reference in [verse] 22 is almost certainly to Christian baptism. . . . The washing of the body with water and the purging of the heart are complementary aspects of Christian conversion."[3] It may surprise the reader, however, that this is not the more popular explanation of the phrase. Donald Guthrie can speak for the dissenting voices: "This appears to be an allusion to Christian baptism, although this view is not without its difficulties. If correct, it would require some initiatory rite of a public nature before anyone could draw near."[4] That is to say, this passage lists "having our bodies washed with pure water" as one of the prerequisites to entering the presence of God. If that's baptism, it means no one gets close to God without the practice of that sacrament. It seems completely out of step with the theology of Hebrews to this point, as nothing of the sort has been previously mentioned. Remember that our author reviewed his theological statements almost to the point of obsession. Why would a church practice suddenly be inserted like that one while he reiterated everything he had taught up to that point?

John MacArthur says this phrase "does not refer to baptism, but has to do with our living, with how the Holy Spirit changes our lives."[5] As Hebrews has focused on change within the human heart and mind because of the blood of

Christ, this seems much more in line with the thrust of the book than the unprecedented mention of a sacrament.

THE THREE EXHORTATIONS (HEB. 10:22 25)

At last we arrive at the more practical teaching of the book of Hebrews. We begin with three exhortations:

1. "Let us draw near to God" (v. 22). This is what we came for, in a manner of speaking. In other words, all that we've learned about the blood and our High Priest has led to this: Get in there. You have access to the Most Holy Place. Go. Be intimate with God.
2. "Let us hold unswervingly to the hope we profess" (v. 23). Although Hebrews 6 mentioned the hope we have (vv. 11, 18, 19), it wasn't distinctly spelled out for us. In context, it is found that our hope is Jesus, as he restores our intended relationship with the Father. There will be those who try to convince us that Jesus himself is not enough. Good works are needed. The intervention of a human priest is needed. But through Jesus alone we approach the throne, and eventually we will be in the complete presence of God.
3. "Let us consider how we may spur one another on toward love and good deeds" (10:24). We people of

the church often fail miserably at this. We are supposed to inspire each other and cheer each other on, but we are great at resenting each other. We resent each other's talents, money, possessions, and position. When we get along well, sometimes we are better at leading each other into temptation than prompting one another to good deeds and love.

Consider the following typical conversation between two believers.

Sister 1: "I just met Karl. He seems like a great guy."

Sister 2: "I'm glad you like him. I've actually seen another side of him, but I'm sure he's grown up since then."

At this point, Sister 1 has a choice of where to take this. She can say, "Yeah, I guess he must have, because he seems like a straight-up kinda guy." Or she can say, "What do you mean?"

If she opts for the second question, Sister 2, who has already crossed a line, has a chance to redeem the conversation by saying, "I spoke out of turn. Let's change the subject." But here's how it usually goes:

Sister 1: "What do you mean? What do you know about Karl that I don't know?"

Sister 2: "I really shouldn't say."

Sister 1: "Oh no, you can't stop now. Come on, you can't start it and not finish it!"

Sister 2: "OK, well, I don't want to gossip, but . . ."

As you can see, there were many points in this conversation where they both could have turned the tide. But that's not always what happens. Instead of helping each other be our most God-honoring selves, we can easily lead each other into sinful behavior.

As subpoints to spurring one another on, our author said we must not neglect meeting together and encouraging one another if we are to promote loving, good deeds in one another. Lone Ranger Christianity does not work. It is a fundamental truth of the church that we were designed to function as a body (see 1 Cor. 12). Anyone who thinks he or she can be a fully functioning Christian without becoming part of the life of the body does not understand what it means to be a follower of Christ. Indeed, a significant portion of the New Testament teaches Christians how to treat each other. Obviously, we are expected to live as a community.

THE DAY APPROACHING (HEB. 10:25)

"The Day" refers, of course, to the coming of the Lord that will mark the end of human history as we know it. When the author of Hebrews reflected on that future moment, he associated it with judgment (see 4:13; 6:2; 9:27). Hebrews doesn't shy away from the notion that even believers must be diligent or they will find themselves in a bad position before the Lord. Here again, a stern warning lies at the center of the writer's exhortation: The day is coming, so don't cease doing what you are meant to do. Judgment approaches.

REFLECTION QUESTIONS

1. What is the significance of the curtain tearing at the moment of Jesus' death? How does this match up with what you've learned in Hebrews?

2. Most of us have heard mythological stories about the gods and goddesses of the ancient Greeks and Romans. In a society that believed in such gods, how do you think the idea of drawing near to God would be received?

3. Do you think the average person on the street today believes that we have the means of being in an intimate relationship with God?

4. In what ways do you draw near to God?

5. Has any other teaching ever caused you to swerve away from the hope we profess?

6. How has a brother or sister in the Lord ever encouraged you or spurred you on to good deeds? Can you think of someone who might need similar spurring from you right now?

7. How is your church and/or Bible study attendance? At the end of the day, we all do what matters most to us. If

you look at the things on your schedule, can you discern what you value most?

8. If we are not to give up meeting together, how much church involvement does God expect from us? Think of things that Christians use as alternatives to fellowship and worship in a church setting. Do the alternatives fulfill the requirement of Hebrews 10:25? Why or why not?

9. Why do you think the author sometimes reminded believers of impending judgment?

23

CHOOSING TO SIN

HEBREWS 10:26–31

DELIBERATE SIN (HEB. 10:26–27)

We've talked about the difference between intentional and unintentional sin, and I've suggested that the majority of Christians do, after salvation, continue to commit willful sins. We say something cruel, fully aware that we are hurting someone's feelings. We cheat on an exam—just a little. We lose our temper with our children instead of pulling back.

I've also stressed the idea that the ultimate sacrifice of the blood of Jesus isn't fully understood if we deny its power to keep us from deliberate sin. Titus 2:11–12 says, "The grace of God has appeared that offers salvation to all people. It teaches us to say 'No' to ungodliness and worldly passions, and to live self-controlled, upright and godly lives." But as we know, not every believer has come to the point where he or she habitually says no to ungodliness and worldly passions. Some—maybe most—still choose to sin at times.

So, what does Hebrews 10:26 mean when it says, "If we deliberately keep on sinning after we have received the knowledge of the truth, no sacrifice for sins is left"? Does this mean that anyone who sins after receiving the blood of Christ is left to face "a fearful expectation of judgment and of raging fire" (v. 27)?

Let's sort out a couple of things. This is a difficult passage, and there are differing interpretations, but let us see if we can reach what seems a fair understanding.

First, we must understand the phrase "deliberately keep on sinning" as it is used in this verse. William Lane describes it as "intentional persistence in sin."[1] In describing the Greek verb used, Kevin Anderson says that "the present tense participle 'keep on sinning' . . . conveys the sense of continuous or persistent sinning."[2] So, this isn't occasionally succumbing to sin. This is a choice to pursue sin as a lifestyle.

Next, let's consider the phrase "received the knowledge of the truth." John MacArthur argues that these verses are about "people whose hearts had been warmed toward the gospel of Christ"[3] but have not made a genuine commitment to Christ. They have not received his blood as their atonement. In contrast, Peter O'Brien says that the phrase "closely resembles a regular expression for conversion in the Pastoral Epistles" and "is consistent with the use of traditional language for conversion in the earlier warning passage of Hebrews 6:4–8."[4] Lane says, "The phrase thus describes a dynamic assimilation of the truth of the gospel. It is an equivalent expression for the solemn description of authentic Christian experience in 6:4–5."[5] So while some commentators think this verse is about people who were never saved in the first place, others think it is about people who were saved but subsequently chose a life of sin over a life dedicated to God.

No explanation is required for the phrase "no sacrifice for sins is left, but only a fearful expectation of judgment and of raging fire." It is painfully clear. I think it is also clear that those who have committed this sin fall into the category of "enemies of God" (10:27).

What the passage seems to say, then, is that this person is not just a Christian who occasionally sins. This is a person who deliberately—though exposed to the gospel truth and the sacrifice of Christ—chooses to commit to sin. Was this person already saved? I think scholars such as O'Brien and Lane offer a convincing argument that this person was.

THE GREATER REJECTION (HEB. 10:28–29)

Those who "rejected the law of Moses" (v. 28) and were killed for it had rejected the law defiantly. They turned up their noses at its authority. But how much more offensive is it to turn your back on the blood of Christ?

A number of years ago, Cuba Gooding Jr. starred in a television movie called *Gifted Hands: The Ben Carson Story*. It was the true story of an impoverished boy who grew to become a famous surgeon. When he was a young teen, he really wanted new clothes. His overworked mother scraped together every penny she could, at great personal sacrifice, and bought him a pair of new pants. But they weren't what he wanted, and he threw a violent fit. It was a heartbreaking scene in the movie because Ben's mother had worked so hard to provide those clothes. She had given all she had to try to help her son save face at school, and he broke her heart.

The Son of God was not without resource, as Ben Carson's mother was, but he gave beyond what anyone could expect. He poured himself out. Our writer offered one of his most vivid images in the book of Hebrews when he wrote that the apostate has "trampled the Son of God under foot" (v. 29). It is even hard to read this sentence, for this person "has treated as an unholy thing the blood of the covenant that sanctified them, and . . . has insulted the Spirit of grace" (v. 29). How could anyone be so cruel, to know that Christ spilled his blood for that person and that the Spirit has showered grace on him or her, and yet trample on that? Apparently at this point, even God reaches his limit, because "no sacrifice for sins is left" (v. 26) for this rebellious, foolish soul.

THE SCARY STUFF (HEB. 10:30–31)

We struggle with the harsh words this writer penned. And yet, this is the Word of God. We are uncomfortable with concepts like vengeance and judgment. We don't want to hear about falling into the hands of God when he is angry. But how could God tolerate the sacrifice of Jesus being trampled upon?

We cannot simply design a God with whom we are comfortable. We have a spectacular, glorious God. He is perfect in every way. As the humans he created, it is our role to submit ourselves to all that he is, even if we find it hard to understand certain things about him. We must trust that all he does is right and just and holy. But since we've also been invited to enjoy intimacy with him, we have opportunity to know him and cherish him.

REFLECTION QUESTIONS

1. Would you agree with MacArthur that only people who aren't truly saved could purposefully devote themselves to sin, or do you agree that these people are "enemies of God" because they received Christ's blood and then deliberately abused it?

2. We are so comfortable with a loving God. Does your picture of God also make room for his exacting justice?

3. What do you think would lead a person to turn his or her back on the salvation of Jesus Christ in a calculated, purposeful way?

4. Why do you think the writer warns his audience about this?

5. Try to write a description of God, in a few sentences, that balances his love with his justice.

24

NOT SHRINKING BACK

HEBREWS 10:32–39

WITHSTANDING THE HARD TIMES (HEB. 10:32–35)

Hebrews offers a lot of encouragement to remain faithful. Sometimes the verbiage is so strong, it sounds more like a threat—as it did in 10:26–31. It seems that the recipients of this letter were beginning to lose heart, and our writer was going to do all he could to keep them in the fold.

I remember when my first child was born. The moment he was put in my arms I felt a stronger love than I'd ever known. My whole world changed, and it was wonderful. Over time, the care of a baby began to wear on me. That kid had *demands*. I had to nurse him every couple of hours. He went through diapers at a rate I hadn't anticipated. Sometimes he cried and cried and I couldn't figure out why. We couldn't go to a movie at the drop of a hat as we could before. My love for him didn't wane, but I really wanted a break.

Perhaps that's how it was for these early Christians. The faith they eagerly embraced turned out to be more demanding than they thought it would be. They had been insulted, persecuted, and their possessions had been confiscated. Friends had been imprisoned, and they had supported them. They probably still understood the value of their faith, but they were growing tired. Maybe they missed the ease of their old life. The writer saw that some of them might give up soon.

The writer asked his recipients not to give up their "confidence" (v. 35), which can also be translated as "boldness." He assured them they would be rewarded. God would not let their abusers have the final word.

I have ideas about how I'd like the Lord to reward me! A nice financial cushion would be a great reward. An unusually high metabolism would be another. Annual passes to Disneyland would be more than acceptable. These are the kinds of rewards that occur to me. But the rewards I've received are on a completely different level. A palpable sense of the Lord's presence is one of the best rewards I've ever known. A sense of peace in a tough situation and protection from harm are other rewards. And some day I will enjoy eternal versions of these rewards. You will too. We will be in the Lord's presence. We will see him with our own eyes, and we will know complete peace and be free from the threat of harm.

WHY PERSEVERE? (HEB. 10:36–39)

It is the will of God that his people persevere in the faith. In addition, perseverance is a requirement for fulfilling other aspects of God's will. If God desired the recipients of Hebrews to evangelize a certain city, his wish would be unfulfilled if they left the faith. If they stayed true, honoring God's will, they would receive rewards.

The writer was concerned about the behavior of the believers because he was convinced Christ would return soon. Earlier in the tenth chapter, the return of the Lord had seemed to be a threat: don't offend your God, because if you do, when the day comes, falling into his hands will be a terrifying thing. The tone of verses 36–38 sounds much more positive, focusing on what we receive if we do right, rather than our punishment if we do wrong. Ironically, the promise that he is coming without delay (v. 37) is a quote from Habakkuk, wherein Habakkuk foretold the imminent destruction of Israel by the Chaldeans. Could it be that by using this quote the writer sent another, very subtle, warning?

The quotes in verses 37–38 are from Habakkuk 2:3–4 and Isaiah 26:21. There is some reworking of the Old Testament text, but what is important to us here is that the writer of Hebrews used these verses to refer to the final arrival of the Savior and the constancy of those who wait for him. Righteous people will not renege. Those who "shrink back" (10:39) will not please God.

People shrink back from things that frighten them or from things that require too much effort on their part. Although being a Christian can provoke some teasing or snubbing from others, most of us have never experienced true persecution, as the original readers of Hebrews did. Most of us have never been in a situation that could cause genuine bodily harm for the cause of the gospel. Perhaps we should consider how blessed we are and be spurred on toward greater works.

JOINING THE RIGHT TEAM (HEB. 10:39)

We are just about to jump into one of the most famous chapters in the New Testament, the roll call of the faithful in Hebrews 11. In chapter 10, we read about the fate of apostates, and we were warned not to give up. We've been promised good things from God if we don't shrink back. Here, in verse 39, our teacher declared that "we do not belong to those who shrink back and are destroyed." We have a frighteningly clear picture of what happens to those who do shrink back. But don't fear; *we* are not the type who would do that, our writer affirmed.

We're not on the losing team. We're on the winning team. We are on the team with all the people we'll read about in chapter 11. We belong to "those who have faith and are saved" (10:39).

The fate of the turncoats is destruction. The fate of the faithful is salvation. Destruction is a result of abandoning the faith. Being saved is a result of *not* abandoning the faith, which would imply that we must not take salvation for granted. To claim it, you must make it to the end.

Don't be afraid. The salvation you received when you first claimed the blood of Jesus is not hanging by a thread. The writer wanted us to understand, however, that you can't run the other direction from your Savior and expect him to defend you on judgment day. You can't trample the Son of God underfoot and insult the Spirit of grace (v. 29) and consider yourself a member of God's family. The author only declared a truth we've heard since childhood: choices have consequences.

REFLECTION QUESTIONS

1. How do you feel about the early Christians who were ready to give in? If you put yourself in their situation, do you think you'd feel the same?

2. Have you ever wanted to give up on your faith or on some specific task God asked you to do? What was the situation, and why did you want to give up?

3. Do you think the reward promised to the believers was for this life or the next?

4. What does a description like "richly rewarded" (v. 35) imply in our day and age? What kind of reward would people expect?

5. What other rewards do you think God offers in this age? What eternal reward do you look forward to?

6. What person's perseverance in doing God's will has directly impacted your life? How?

7. Think of someone in recent history whose life has been in danger because of the gospel. Would you have been brave enough to take on his or her role if God had asked? Are you brave enough today?

8. What is the closest you have come to feeling persecuted for your faith? How did you handle the situation?

9. Some say that those who shrink back were never saved in the first place. Others say that they are saved believers who abandon their faith. Based on what we've been studying in Hebrews 10, what do you say? It may help to also refer to Hebrews 3:7–19 (devotion 8) and 6:4–19 (devotion 12).

25

ROLL CALL OF THE FAITHFUL, PART 1

HEBREWS 11:1–16

WHAT IS FAITH? (HEB. 11:1–3)

When we looked at Hebrews 10, we talked about rewards. There are rewards on this earth for following Christ, but the greater rewards are those that await us. The things we haven't yet experienced will far outweigh what we know now. We hold on to this truth not because we can prove it, but because we have faith. Faith is feeling confident, not doubting the reality of what we can't see. This is how the author defines faith for us. Then he gives us an example: No one saw God create the earth, but we believe he did it. That is an act of faith.

I am writing this a few days after a snowstorm where I live. Because Northern Virginia isn't well equipped for a lot of snow, people here like to be prepared before it comes.

It is important to know in advance if we are going to get more than a dusting. So, we listen to our weather reporters. They show us weather patterns and explain how factors will combine to produce our weather conditions. They predict, with pretty good accuracy, how much snow we might get.

Although the weather reporters aren't perfectly precise, we put a lot of trust in what they say. We have faith because they show us the indicators. We also have faith because they've been right before. We have good reason to believe them. Some of our biblical heroes had reason to believe God, but some did not. Abraham (Abram at the time), for example, trusted God and did as he said, even though God had no proven track record with him yet. He just trusted. Other great heroes of the faith had seen the hand of God in the lives of the Israelite tribes and perhaps in their own lives. Still, a leap of faith was required when God asked them to do something new and unexpected.

The important thing is that these people obeyed the will of God without guarantee. I often say that I would leap off any cliff just to feel God catch me. I know how sweet that moment is, when he catches me and shows me why he had me jump out in faith. But honestly, when my toes are at the edge of that cliff and I'm looking down, it is a terrifying moment.

Like the readers of Hebrews, we have a Book full of examples of God's faithfulness when people were faithful to him. Because we are encouraged when we hear of God's faithfulness to others, the writer provided us with a long list.

THE DEEDS OF THE FAITHFUL, PART 1 (HEB. 11:4–12)

Let's look at the list of faithful people from verses 4–12. Here is a simple chart reviewing their faithfulness.

PERSON	FAITHFUL ACT	RESULT
Abel	God-honoring sacrifice.	God's approval; we still learn from Abel's appropriate sacrifice.
Enoch	Pleased God.	Taken to heaven without dying.
Noah	Built an ark. Condemned the world (which could refer either to the fact that Noah preached repentance to the world, or that his own righteous living "constitute[d] a rebuke to a godless generation"[1]).	Became an heir of right-eousness; he has become a model for us all, and will share with us in reaping the rewards of faithfulness.
Abraham	Left his home and lived as a stranger in a foreign land.	Became the ancestral parent of a great nation.
Sarah	Believed in God's promise of a child.	Bore a child in her old age; became the ancestral parent of a great nation.

These are all very well-known Bible stories. The faith of these great people is something we still speak about thousands of years later. That in itself is some sort of reward. Wouldn't you feel honored if people were still telling the story of your faithfulness thousands of years from now?

WHAT WAS NOT RECEIVED (HEB. 11:13–16)

Almost everyone relates to Job at some point in his or her life. You remember Job, who started out rich and happy, but was dealt blow after devastating blow, from the death of his children to painful boils all over his skin. The great thing about the story of Job is its happy ending. Retaining his faith through all he endured, "the LORD blessed the latter part of Job's life more than the former part" (Job 42:12). He had new kids, much more wealth, and lived a long life.

But it doesn't always happen that way. Don't you know of righteous, faithful people who struggle their whole lives? These people may have a joyful spirit, but we look at them and wonder why they aren't more blessed. Maybe they spend their lives caring for a child with a medical or psychological disorder. Maybe they never rise above the poverty line. Maybe they are severely injured as a result of a bad automobile accident.

Maybe we even look at our own lives and wonder why *we* aren't more blessed.

The great heroes of the faith in Hebrews 11 didn't live to see the fulfillment of what they'd been promised. The best example of this is Abraham and Sarah. They still lived in tents, never seeing a permanent settlement built. They had a son, but they never saw the abundant progeny God promised.

Many honored persons of biblical history, who followed God in extreme circumstances, did not see their reward before death. But this should not discourage us! Although Abraham and Sarah never saw the promises fulfilled, we know that they were, and that ancient couple will be with us in eternity, reaping the rewards of faithfulness. You and I may not find the blessings of Job in our lives. But can we not commit ourselves to God's timetable, knowing that he always follows through when he deems best?

God is smarter than we are. We may feel it is in our best interest to reap a little reward now, but God knows otherwise. Think on that for a few moments. Take a moment to write a short prayer, asking the Holy Spirit to help you persevere even when you don't see rewards for it.

Verses 15–16 tell us that the ancient heroes were not looking back to what they had left behind. They had their sights set on a "better country—a heavenly one" (v. 16). Gareth Cockerill says, "The preacher uses the word 'better' throughout Hebrews (6:9; 7:19, 22; 8:6; 9:23; 10:34, 11:35, 40; 12:24) to describe the work of Christ, fully sufficient and effective in redeeming us from sin, and the eternal blessings that come from that work. 'Better' does not contrast with what is 'good,' but with what is temporary, ineffective, weak, and useless."[2]

At the end of the day, most of us would prefer to have what is eternal instead of what is temporary, ineffective, weak, and useless. Like the ancients, we should be "longing for a better country" (11:16). The result of this faithful attitude is wonderful: God was not ashamed to call himself the God of Abraham and Sarah and Noah. On top of that, the eternal city was awaiting them. Aren't those the things we really want too?

REFLECTION QUESTIONS

1. When has God required you to exercise great faith? What was the result?

2. Which of the faithful heroes reviewed in verses 4–12 is your favorite? Why does that person appeal to you?

3. What is God's attitude toward faithful people (v. 16)? What does this mean in relationship to you?

26

ROLL CALL OF THE FAITHFUL, PART 2

HEBREWS 11:17–31

THE DEEDS OF THE FAITHFUL, PART 2 (HEB. 11:17–31)

The list of heroes and their faithful deeds continues.

PERSON	FAITHFUL ACT	RESULT
Abraham	Offered his son as a sacrifice.	Isaac was received back from "the dead."
Isaac	Blessed his sons.	
Jacob	Blessed Joseph's sons; worshiped in his old age.	
Joseph	Prophesied that God would lead his children out of Egypt.	

continued

PERSON	FAITHFUL ACT	RESULT
Moses' parents	Protected Moses from the slaughter of baby boys (Ex. 1:15–22) by hiding him.	
Moses	Chose to live as an Israelite rather than a grandson of the pharaoh; boldly left Egypt; kept the Passover.	
Israelites	Passed through the Red Sea; marched around the walls of Jericho.	Survived when Pharaoh's army drowned; saw the walls of Jericho fall.
Rahab	Welcomed Israelite spies.	Life was spared.

REMARKABLE COURAGE (HEB. 11:17–19)

Perhaps the most courageous, faithful act in the Bible (besides Christ offering himself) is that of Abraham's sacrifice of Isaac. God had promised more descendants than stars in the sky, and Isaac was the vehicle for the fulfillment of that promise. In fact, in Genesis 21:12, God said to Abraham, "It is through Isaac that your offspring will be reckoned."

How much did Abraham struggle with God's command? How could he bear to carry out the sacrifice of his son, and how could he continue to believe in the promise? Here's an interesting thought: "Surprisingly, neither the Genesis narrative nor the account in Hebrews dwells on the inner turmoil within Abraham's heart. In fact, the impression one gets is that Abraham regarded it as God's problem."[1]

It is hard to imagine that Abraham could be so trusting that he would just calmly go about the bone-chilling business. And yet, it seems as if that is what happened. According to Hebrews, Abraham thought God had the power to raise someone from the dead. Abraham had never seen such a thing happen. But he knew. He just *knew* that God would not go back on his promise. If Isaac was to be an ancestor to the great nation, then God would do something. God doesn't renege on his promises.

Can you imagine methodically assembling the altar, wondering when God would step in? Would he stop you once you'd stacked the wood? Would he stop you once you'd tied down your son? Would he make you follow through, and raise your son from the dead?

Maybe you are in a situation where you believe that God will step in, but he seems to delay so long. You wait and wait for him to come to your rescue. You know he is able. But is he willing? When will he come?

The answer, of course, is that God always comes. He always rescues his people. He just doesn't always do it in the way we expect or as quickly as we'd like.

MOSES (HEB. 11:23–28)

The story of Moses is remarkable from the very beginning. Scholars say that his parents looked at him and saw that he had physical features of nobility. This is what is meant by "they saw he was no ordinary child" (v. 23). It is likely that these fine features helped ease his way into the royal household after Pharaoh's daughter discovered him floating in a basket in the Nile.

Apparently Moses never fully identified with the Egyptians. Maybe his biological mother, who served as his wet nurse, whispered his true identity to him. For whatever reasons, he chose to join the enslaved Israelites, considering them his brothers.

The story of Moses goes on. A strange comment in this text is that Moses "regarded disgrace for the sake of Christ" (v. 26). Moses would not have known Jesus, obviously. Nor would he have even heard prophecies of a coming Savior. Why would the author of Hebrews write this?

"Like Christ, Moses exchanged the joy he could have had for the endurance of hardship with the people of God."[2] The author's intent here was to associate Moses with Christ. Moses made similar choices to Christ's, and we are to do the same, viewing Christ and Moses as our models. Why did Moses leave the pleasures of Egypt for the hardships of the desert? Because, like the other heroes listed, he was willing to give up one country for a better one (11:15–16). You will remember that by "better" the author meant "eternal" (see devotion 25). Moses opted for greater, eternal reward over temporary, earthly pleasure.

REFLECTION QUESTIONS

1. How has God come to your aid in unexpected ways?

2. Why do you think God is pleased when we trust that he has things under control?

3. As God called Moses, imagine God called you to spend the rest of your life as a missionary in a remote land., What would you find difficult to give up?

4. Rather than giving up things, we often focus on what we'd like to acquire. In the past few days, have you remarked on or thought about something you wished you could have?

5. Find something you have that you are willing to give away today—something that you actually like. As you make your small sacrifice, identify with the sacrifice of Christ and all of the saints who have gone before us, putting the rewards of following the will of God above all else.

PART 6

THE FINAL
OUTCOME

HEBREWS 11:32—13:25

27

ULTIMATE VICTORY, ULTIMATE UNITY

HEBREWS 11:31—12:3

HEROES WHO WON AND HEROES WHO LOST
(HEB. 11:32–39)

As the writer listed more heroes and more situations, he included two types of faithful people: those who found earthly victory, and those who will find victory only in the next life.

The names of Gideon, Barak, and David appear early in the list. These men conquered kingdoms, administered justice, and gained political victories that had been promised to them. We can easily recognize the reference to Daniel as the one "who shut the mouths of lions" (v. 33), and Shadrach, Meshach and Abednego as those who survived the flames. Many Old Testament characters escaped the sword: David, Elijah, Elisha, and so on. Samson's weakness was turned to strength.

Many were successful in battle. And the pinnacle of the events listed is mentioned last: women who had lost someone to death saw them rise. Both Elijah and Elisha raised a widow's son from death. All of these spectacular events came to pass because of the faith of the people involved.

Then the list changes direction, from those who "won" to those who didn't. There were many faithful people, similar to Abraham and Sarah, who did not see promises fulfilled. In fact, they suffered immensely.

The list of those who experienced miracles climaxed with the women whose dead were raised. But verse 35 tells us the sufferers of the upcoming list endured their pain so that they might obtain a *better* resurrection. When the widows' sons were raised, it was temporary. They would die again. But the better resurrection is eternal.

Some heroes of the faith were tortured and refused to be released in order to gain the better resurrection. They would have had to recant their faith to be released. But if they wanted God to find them faithful, they had to endure. Some were insulted, beaten, chained, and thrown into prison; and some were even killed. The stoning may be a reference to the legend that Jeremiah was stoned in Egypt. Legend also taught that Isaiah was sawn in two.

The list of heroes who "lost" in this life concludes with believers who were so destitute that they wore animal skins and lived in caves. John the Baptist springs to mind. But in the end, all the people listed—both those who knew success and those who experienced great loss—were "commended for their faith." And none of them, even those who found victory, "received what had been promised" (v. 39).

We know what had been promised, as we have dealt with it in previous devotions. These early men and women of faith received neither the better covenant nor the better mediator. They did not have the full cleansing from sin and the access to the throne of God that came through the sacrifice of Jesus Christ. If they could be faithful before those benefits came into play, it seems we should find it easier to be faithful.

MADE PERFECT TOGETHER (HEB. 11:40)

While we are already benefactors of the new covenant and the ancient heroes were not, God decided that "only together with us would they be made perfect" (v. 40). We are perfect in that we are cleansed by the blood of Christ and able to be in the presence of God.

"Those people of faith experience this reality only 'together with us,' we who live after Christ. We cannot be precise in determining the degree to which they by faith in God's promise participated in the benefits of Christ before He came. But now, they partake fully 'together with us' of all those benefits."[1]

THE WITNESSES (HEB. 12:1)

The cloud of witnesses consists of all the saints before us, represented by the people listed in the roll call of the faithful. While we cannot say for certain whether the people who went before us can actually observe us, they are certainly witnesses in the sense that their lives gave testimony (witness) to what it means to be faithful.

With such great testimonies to observe, we must take them as our models. We must free ourselves from anything that would distract us from our goal. We must live free of any sin that would trip us up.

I'm certainly no athlete. But I have been to physical therapy, where I had to do an exercise I found very demanding. I was instructed to keep my eyes forward and look at a decades-old picture of Joe Namath, former football star, that hung on the wall. If I focused on him, I would perform the exercise better. I would joke with the therapist about how my "ol' buddy Joe" was getting me through. I called him my inspiration. In the same way, as we run our race with perseverance, we are to keep our eyes fixed on Jesus. A fixed gaze keeps us focused and inspired.

PIONEER AND PERFECTER (HEB. 12:2)

What we see that is new in this verse is the idea that "for the joy set before him he endured the cross" (v. 2). The cross was endured for our salvation, so it follows that our salvation is Jesus' joy! He loves us so much!

The writer asked us to think of Jesus, who gave up so much for us. By meditating on him and his strength through suffering, we will assume the same courage Christ had. Not only does Christ give us hope, he gives us the strength and boldness we need to endure. And we must endure to the end.

REFLECTION QUESTIONS

1. Were those who suffered and died more faithful than those who reached a point of triumph in their lives? Why or why not?

2. Do you think the people on the winners list were denied the better resurrection? Do you have to die a martyr's death to receive it?

3. Think about your life. Can you describe the race you are running? Are you on a smooth path right now, or are you in a rocky spot?

4. Imagine that someone were to summarize the highlights of your faith journey. You most likely haven't endured

a fiery furnace or been flogged. What do you think your biographer would say were your major moments?

5. How do you think focusing on Jesus helps us run the race better?

6. What practical things must we do to keep our eyes fixed on Jesus?

7. Describe a time when fixing your eyes on Jesus resulted in overcoming your difficulties. How has that experience grown your faith?

28

THE BENEFITS OF DISCIPLINE
HEBREWS 12:4–12

GOD'S DISCIPLINE (HEB. 12:4–11)

The "struggle against sin" mentioned in verse 4 is not fighting off one's temptation to do wrong. Here, "sin" represents people who wish to defame and harm believers. The recipients of this letter have certainly encountered such people, but they have not been abused to the point they've been seriously injured or martyred.

It is interesting, and perhaps a little unsettling, that God's plan for disciplining his children involves abuse from those outside the faith. The believer on the receiving end of that abuse is to find comfort in the words of Proverbs 3:11–12, which says not to lose heart when he God rebukes you. The believer is to receive the hardship as God's own correction.

Scripture isn't clear as to whether or not God *prompts* unbelievers to persecute Christians so that they may be disciplined, although such things did occur in the Old Testament. For instance, God exacted his judgment on Israel by sending nations to conquer the people of Israel. However, this kind of disciplinary action seems unlikely under the new covenant. It makes sense to assume that although God *uses* maltreatment to chasten his children, he doesn't *cause* it.

The greatest encouragement in this passage is that God considers us his children. Discipline is a loving act from a father who wants to help his children be the best they can be. Those who aren't disciplined aren't "true sons and daughters" (Heb. 12:8). I have many friends with children and teenagers. I care very much about my friends' kids. I might guide them when appropriate. I might give advice if asked. But I don't discipline my friends' kids, because they aren't mine. That is their parents' responsibility.

As parents, my husband and I have made many discipline mistakes. We've been too lenient; we've been too firm. The problem is, we can't see inside our kids' heads, and we are incapable of knowing every fact of every situation. We do the best we can with the information we have. How different it is with God! He knows everything. His discipline, therefore, is always exactly what we need. We won't enjoy it, for "no discipline seems pleasant at the time." But when we allow ourselves to be molded by it, "it produces a harvest of righteousness and peace" (v. 11).

How does this passage apply to those of us who aren't under threat of physical persecution? The basic situation the book of Hebrews addresses is that unbelievers are pressing in on believers, making their lives difficult. Most likely, the goal of the unbelievers is to make the believers abandon their faith. That's why the writer pleaded with the people to endure.

It is common even today for a believer to feel pressured to abandon his or her faith. We are told our religion is intolerant. Sometimes we are told it is full of fables. We live in a post-Christian era, and the heat is intensifying. In some places, we are looked upon with a wary eye if we admit that we are Christians. The tenets of our faith, they say, are outdated, bigoted, and ignorant.

God uses these situations to discipline us. Discipline isn't only punishment. "The Greek word translated 'discipline' is a bit broader than the English word. Ancient writers used it to describe the training of children. It includes both instruction and correction."[1]

When we feel misunderstood and mocked, God uses that abuse to help us solidify where we stand. He strengthens us so we will stay true, even though it hurts.

SHARING IN GOD'S HOLINESS (HEB. 12:10)

The ultimate purpose of the discipline is that we "may share in his holiness" (v. 10). This is a startling phrase. We've been talking about holy living in this book, but what does it mean to actually share in God's holiness?

Let us consider this phrase as two-pronged. First, it is God's desire that we should be like him. We model ourselves after Jesus, who is righteous and blameless. As God disciplines us, he smoothes our rough edges. He sculpts us into an image that more and more resembles Christ.

Second, this is an invitation to be part of the holy life of God. It means that even while we are on this earth, we have an investment in what is eternal, and we will someday enjoy that to its fullest. We have access to the throne now, but someday we will be in his complete presence, and we will enter into divine rest, as we learned in Hebrews 4.[2]

STRONG TOGETHER (HEB. 12:12–13)

One of my teenage sons actually leaves the house at 4:45 a.m. several times a week. His friend picks him up, and they go to the gym to lift weights. He absolutely loves it, and I admire his tenacity. I, however, passionately hate going to the physical therapy gym where I must go a few days a week. It is one thing when you are strong and you are working out to get stronger. Apparently, that's kind of fun. But it is another thing when you have been injured and are weak, and you must get back to health. It's the injured and weak that we find in Hebrews 12:12.

Those being addressed had suffered. They hadn't yet shed blood, but they were exhausted from the many hardships they had faced because of their faith. They had been running the race, but it wasn't over yet, and they were worn down. They had injuries. But the Lord used the hardships they had known to make them better. They were to be strengthened, knowing that the harvest of righteousness and peace was being produced.

This section is rounded off by a beautiful exhortation to assist the brothers and sisters who are in the worst shape. Level the paths. Smooth out the course. Do what you can to make it easier for those who are truly hurting. They must be healed; they must be able to stay on the path. As fellow Christians, we have something to do with the success of our brothers and sisters! We do not live in silos. We are a unit. William Lane explains verse 13 this way: "The reference is to persons within the house church who have been severely weakened by fatigue, for whom the others are to be genuinely concerned. If those who are stronger will move in a straight direction toward the goal, the brother or sister who is lame will follow more easily and will be healed of his [or her] hurt."[3]

Meghan was a high school student who had made the state championships in track. While running the last lap, she noticed another runner cramping and beginning to fall over. Meghan went to her aid. She wrapped her arm around the other girl and supported her to the finish. As they approached the line, Meghan gently pushed the other girl ahead of her, giving her a higher place than her own. When interviewed, Meghan said, "She worked this hard to get here, so she deserved to finish ahead of me."[4] That selfless concern for the victory of others is exactly what the writer of Hebrews was writing about.

PEACE AND HOLINESS (HEB. 12:14–17)

It is important not to pull verse 14 out of context, otherwise it will be misunderstood. "Live in peace with everyone" is specifically peace with every fellow believer. Hebrews 12:12–16 is a brief passage about our responsibility for each other. It is about unity and spiritual health within the church body. Even holiness has a corporate feel in this passage, as we will see in a moment.

In Hebrews, we have learned that holiness is a gift we've received through Christ, not a reward for our efforts. The word *holiness* speaks of the purity that is ours because of the blood of Christ. Hence, we cannot see the Lord without it. But if holiness is a gift, why would we need to pursue it? We pursue it in the sense that we are to actively maintain it. Some in the church were ready to give up, ready to forfeit the grace of God, ready to "shrink back" (10:39). They were considering exchanging their holy status for the comfort of being accepted by the world. Think of what we've just read—they were constantly pressured to give up their faith. Some were teetering on the edge.

In this passage, holiness is the responsibility of both the individual and the Christian community. The next few verses instruct the strong to care for the weak, just as the preceding few verses exhorted. "See to it that no one falls short of the grace of God" (12:15) is an awfully big assignment. A great deal of diligence is required here. This is Christian accountability, and we can't do it without investing time and an abundance of love.

The church (the people, not just the staff) is responsible to prevent believers from rejecting the holy status they have gained through Jesus' grace. We must not allow bitterness to take root. Believers need to demand sexual purity from each other.

Why is all of this important? Esau shows us why. Esau gave up his birthright for a meal because he was hungry, miserable, and tired. Once he sold his birthright, he could not regain it, no matter how much he regretted having sold it. Esau gave up what mattered so that he might enjoy immediate gratification. This was considered "godless" (v. 16). Should the faithful become apostates, rejecting the grace of God so that they might escape persecution and have an easier life, then "no sacrifice for sins is left" (10:26). This is obviously an extreme case, but the recipients of Hebrews were nearly at that point. We, too, imitate Esau's godless behavior if we opt for the temporary pleasure that comes from sexual immorality, or value even the secret pleasure of nurturing bitterness over the commitment to our holiness. We must keep each other in check so this doesn't happen.

REFLECTION QUESTIONS

1. Have you ever encountered a situation in which you felt uncomfortable because you were a believer? Have you ever felt pressure to abandon what you believe?

2. In what ways is God sculpting you at this stage of your life? Are there any bad habits or attitudes he is chipping away? What godly characteristics does he seem to be developing in you now? Is this experience painful for you?

3. What do you consider to be the benefits of God's discipline?

4. Who has encouraged you in your faith and let you lean on them through the tough times?

5. In your church life, are there some who see to it that no one falls short of the grace of God? Is your church set up for that kind of accountability?

6. Do you bristle at the idea of having someone closely monitor your life? If so, why?

7. Is there someone you know who needs to be supported in his or her Christian walk? Are you strong enough to be that support?

8. Would you be willing to lovingly confront a brother or sister who is beginning to stray? How do you think you can do that appropriately?

29

MOUNT SINAI AND MOUNT ZION

HEBREWS 12:18–28

CONTRASTING THE MOUNTAINS (HEB. 12:18–24)

If you haven't yet appreciated how blessed you are to live under the new covenant, reread the first paragraph of this passage. The writer described Mount Sinai, where Moses met with God. Only Moses was allowed. Any other person— or even an animal—would have to be killed if he or she or it came into contact with that concentration of the holiness of God. If you and I had been there, we would not have been able to talk with God as we do now. Nor would we want to! We would revere him, but we would probably live in fear of him.

But we have not come to Mount Sinai. We have come to Mount Zion.

King David made his home on Mount Zion, and he kept the ark of the covenant there, as well. His son Solomon built the temple just north of Zion, and, of course, the ark was then housed in the temple. This entire area was within the city of Jerusalem. Jerusalem and Mount Zion became very symbolic: It was where God dwelt, and it was the focus point of all the tribes of Israel.

Mount Zion is also referred to in an eschatological[1] sense. "As the earthly Zion was the meeting point for the tribes of the old Israel, so the heavenly Zion is the meeting point for the new Israel."[2] Hebrews 12 refers to the heavenly Zion. We may not be there yet, but we are already citizens of it.

Our Mount Zion, home of the living God, houses great numbers of angels. Verse 23 says it is also home to "the church of the firstborn." In Hebrews 1:6, Jesus was referred to as the firstborn. It is a term of status, because the first-born was the one with the inheritance rights. Just as Jesus was the firstborn Son of God, so we also are inheritors of all that God has to offer, children of God and brothers and sisters of Christ. We were reminded in 12:16–17 that Esau became godless, foregoing his birthright for immediate comfort. Those who will enter heavenly Mount Zion as firstborn children of the church will have clutched tightly to their birthright as grace-born children of God.

WHEN WE GET THERE (HEB. 12:22–24)

In our eschatological home, here's whom we will encounter:

- "Thousands upon thousands of angels in joyful assembly" (v. 22).
- "God, the Judge of all" (v. 23).
- "The spirits of the righteous made perfect" (v. 23).
- "Jesus the mediator of a new covenant" (v. 24).

All the righteous beings of all ages will gather together in that heavenly Mount Zion. Our timeless God will be before our eyes. We will hear the praises of the angels who have already been in his presence acknowledging his glory. "The spirits of the righteous made perfect" are those who have died, who were made perfect by the blood of Christ, whether they lived under the old covenant or the new (see Heb. 11:39–40). And our Savior, who perfected us and enabled us to enter the heavenly Zion, will be in our midst. This is our happy future.

It is the "sprinkled blood" of Christ that has given us this future. Verse 24 compares that blood to Abel's. Abel's blood cried out from the grave (Gen. 4:10). Because of that cry, his murder was avenged. How vastly different is the blood of Christ—offered up, not taken—that was accompanied by his cry, "Father, forgive them."

THE SHAKEDOWN (HEB. 12:25–29)

As God spoke on Mount Sinai, he also speaks to the people living under the new covenant. But if those who refused him under the old covenant were punished, what can we say about those who have heard his voice from heaven but turn away? These are the people who have believed but are nearing the point of abandonment. This is a persistent concern with the writer of Hebrews. Much of the third section of the book was written in an effort to prevent apostasy.

We read in Hebrews 10:28–29, "Anyone who rejected the law of Moses died without mercy on the testimony of two or three witnesses. How much more severely do you think someone deserves to be punished who has trampled the Son of God underfoot, who has treated as an unholy thing the blood of the covenant that sanctified them, and who has insulted the Spirit of grace?"

In ancient times, the Lord's voice shook the earth. The writer described the final judgment day, when again God's voice will shake earth and also the heavens. He will remove what can be shaken, and only what is true will remain.

When I was a child, my parents took my siblings and me to an old mining town that was revitalized for tourists. While there, we had the chance to pan for gold. We took our trays to the stream and filled them with water and sand.

There were holes in the bottom of the pan, and when we shook them the sand exited the pan and anything left was (supposedly) real gold. It sounds as though judgment day won't be much different. God will shake, shake, shake, and what is not in an eternal relationship with him will drift away. Only what is eternal will remain.

The kingdom of God, of which we are citizens through the blood of Christ, cannot be shaken. God is a consuming fire, and fire purifies. Because he is such a mighty fire, we are to "be thankful, and so worship God acceptably" (12:28). Take a moment now to express your thanks and worship to God.

REFLECTION QUESTIONS

1. Why do you think Mount Sinai had to be so terrifying?

2. Why is our experience with God personal and not terrifying?

3. What is in store for those who "refuse him who speaks" (v. 25)?

4. What is in store for those who listen and obey?

30

LOVE AND SECURITY

HEBREWS 13:1–8

INTRODUCTORY THOUGHT

With devotion 22 (beginning with Heb. 10:19), we entered the section of Hebrews that I've called "The Practical Implications" of holiness. So far, all that is practical has been presented through the lens of theology. The tone changes with Hebrews 13. Like other New Testament Epistles, the writer ends with a set of instructions for appropriate Christian living, and the theological background is minimal. As we read the instructions, let us remember the foundation on which they rest, especially the injunctions to live in peace and hold one another accountable for holy living.

THE NEEDS OF OTHERS (HEB. 13:1–3)

Holy living requires emulating Christ. As we've seen throughout the book of Hebrews, Christ put his own glory aside and made our need his first priority. We honor Christ when we also put others first. Three simple instructions are given toward that end:

1. "Keep on loving one another as brothers and sisters" (v. 1).
2. "Show hospitality to strangers" (v. 2).
3. "Remember those in prison . . . and those who are mistreated" (v. 3).

A few years ago, I witnessed an act of brotherly love that truly moved me. The car of a college student at our church broke down, and she couldn't afford to repair it. One of the men at our church went to the library, researched how to repair her car, bought the parts and whatever tools he didn't already have, and fixed it himself. That's a lot of effort. That's genuine Christian love.

Hospitality is another expression of Christian love. It was particularly important at the time this epistle was written. If a person was traveling, it could be dangerous to stay at an inn. It was important, therefore, for believers to provide food and shelter for other believers who were traveling or otherwise in need, not only for the benefit of fellowship, but to keep them safe. The remark that the strangers might actually be angels is quite engaging and has biblical precedent in Genesis 18–19. Perhaps you have had an encounter with a stranger that you subsequently believed might have been an angel. It is intriguing to think that we could have a physical interaction with a representative from the world unseen.

On a much earthier note, however, the author reminded his readers of the believers languishing in prison and others being mistreated. It is very easy to forget those who are out of our sight. Sometimes we remember them initially, but over time we forget them. How easily we forget the images of starving people we see online or on television. How readily we complain over minor inconveniences, when brothers and sisters the world over are persecuted, families have no source of water, and children are forced to be soldiers.

Many Westerners visit orphanages or communities for the maimed in developing nations. While there, they feel a surge of empathy and an urgent need to do something. When they return home, however, the empathy may begin to wane. They become consumed with their own lives.

I thank God that my son refused to extinguish the flame burning in his heart after visiting children's homes in the Caribbean. Though he was only fifteen, he returned home with a conviction that our family should adopt a child. Not quite two years later, we welcomed our two new children from St. Vincent into our family. We are not a perfect family. We are still wasteful and neglectful and self-absorbed, like so many Westerners. My husband and I are trying to teach our children—and ourselves—to deny ourselves some things so that we might be able to provide what others need. It isn't easy, but can anyone deny it is the Christlike thing to do?

There are those who live with tragic need, but there are also those—closer to home, usually—who have an urgent, temporary need. Consider those who worship with you. Is there a single parent who needs a break from the kids? Is there a college student who hasn't had a decent meal all semester? Has someone with a family to feed been laid off?

TWO TEMPTATIONS (HEB. 13:4–5)

If we were to make a list of "Top Ten Temptations," the two problems listed in these verses would likely fill the first and second slots: sex and greed.

The notion that married people should keep sex between themselves was not necessarily a given in the culture and times in which Hebrews was written. Even some rabbis had a "live-and-let-live" attitude toward marital infidelity. Our writer was very direct, letting the readers know how displeasing sexual immorality is to God. God's injunctions are based in love, and adultery or promiscuity is steeped in selfishness and always results in hurt, both for the perpetrators and for their family members. This is true with all types of sexual immorality. The media would have us believe that no one is hurt when two consenting adults have recreational sex together. But we weren't designed for physical acts devoid of emotional connection.

Greed is another kind of lust. It is unbiblical in every way because it revolves around the self. Even those who do altruistic things can be victims of this ugly sin if they seek money for their own desires first. Greed can topple businesses and destroy families. It is a monster whose appetite never wanes. It is because of greed that some people starve while others live in comfort. It is the antithesis of the love and hospitality we are to share.

YOUR NEEDS ARE MET (HEB. 13:5–6)

Rather than pursuing money, we are to be content with what we have. To chase after money is to doubt the security that God provides. To counteract selfishness, quotes are provided from Deuteronomy 31:6 and Psalm 118:6–7. These quotes are something of a surprise, because they aren't specifically about money. And yet, they explain why we should be happy with what we have, and they provide perfect reassurance for the person in financial need: God will not forsake his children. He is our helper, so we have nothing to fear. If you have reason to worry about your finances, remember that God will not leave you! If you are not worried about money, consider whether God might want to use you as his agent to help someone else.

FOLLOW THE EXAMPLE (HEB. 13:7–8)

When the writer told his readers to "remember your leaders who spoke the word of God to you" (v. 7), he was speaking of those leaders who were part of the formation of the church and had since died. As these verses follow instructions on caring for others and avoiding temptation, it stands to reason that the leaders were exemplary in those matters. Therefore, it is suggested that we imitate their lifestyles and their faith.

In Hebrews 11, we reviewed the great heroes of the faith. But not all examples of righteous living are found in the Old Testament. The readers of Hebrews could look back to the men and women they had known who lived righteously. And we may do the same.

REFLECTION QUESTIONS

1. What acts of genuine Christian love have you witnessed?

2. Many Christian organizations offer the opportunity to "adopt a child," that is, to send a monthly check to help with the child's expenses. What other means of helping the needy are you aware of?

3. Make a list of things you could do to help people in need, and determine which one you are going to do. If it is too much for you, ask a friend to help out.

4. You may have been involved in sexual sin, you may have been affected by someone else's sin, or you may have just watched from a distance the harm it does. What damage have you observed as a result of sex outside of marriage?

5. Have you seen the brutality of greed firsthand?

6. Do you struggle with temptation in the area(s) of greed or lust? Based on this devotion, what are some truths you must keep in mind to help you fight these temptations?

7. Why do you think it is so easy for us to worry about money? What messages does society send us about money?

8. Have you ever been in dire financial straits and seen God come through for you? Describe what happened.

9. Name one person you've known who lived a Christian life worth imitating. What made that individual so special?

FINAL WORDS

HEBREWS 13:9–25

CEREMONIAL FOODS AND SACRIFICES (HEB. 13:9–16)

Believers in Christ had no business participating in the longstanding Jewish rituals and the customs that developed around them. "Strange teachings" (v. 9) would attempt to persuade them that they needed to be involved in these things. But the new ways and the old ways could not coexist.

"These various inferior and 'strange' teachings probably involved various 'ceremonial foods' . . . that Jews throughout the Roman world ate in conjunction with certain rituals taking place in the Jerusalem temple."[1] But because the grace of Christ was completely sufficient to cleanse from the inside out, such a custom was of no benefit.

It was customary for certain foods to be eaten from the altar, but Christians now had their own "altar" from which the priests and rejecters of Christ could not partake. This "altar" is the sacrifice of Christ. It is the place where the heart of a person receives the grace of the Savior. The ceremonial food and the altar of Christ were signifiers of the two separate covenants. If one accepted the grace of the new covenant, the other would be of no use.

To the Jewish priests, the region outside the city gate, where the carcasses were burned, was unclean. But it was there in the "unclean" territory that Christ was offered up as sacrifice. It is there that his people are made holy through the blood he shed. His people are to join him in the disgrace of going outside the gate. It is our honor to identify with him in every way. The earthly Jerusalem is of little consequence to us anyway, as we look forward to the heavenly city described in Hebrews 12.

As we stand outside the gate, we offer a sacrifice that has nothing to do with animals. Our sacrifice is one of praise, as we proclaim and adore him with our lips. Through the blood of Jesus and not the blood of a bull, our sacrifice is worthy and good. We add to that our sacrifice of service and sharing. In so doing, we prove our offering is substantial. We don't recite words of empty praise. We demonstrate that we mean what we say by taking care of others, for all humankind is of value to God.

Take a moment to offer a sacrifice of praise. Pray out loud, praising God for who he is, or sing a song of praise.

HONORING LEADERS (HEB. 13:17)

In Hebrews 13:7, the writer admonished his readers to remember and honor their past leaders. Here in verse 17, he gave instruction regarding their current leaders. He told the believers to have confidence in them and submit to their authority.

Everyone knows the old joke about serving up "roast preacher" for lunch on Sunday afternoon. Unfortunately, Christians today can have a very cavalier attitude toward the men and women God has placed in authority. These men and women have additional spiritual responsibility: "They keep watch over you as those who must give an account." They will stand before God and justify the care they have given to you. They are to be honored, not ridiculed. Respected, not mocked.

We don't seem to like the idea of authority in church these days. If we take this verse seriously, we stand chastised. I can imagine the writer looking at us today and saying, "Did I stutter?" The man or woman at the helm of a group of believers has received a holy calling. That is not to say that your mission at the office or on campus or in the neighborhood isn't as critical as theirs. All of us are called to serve and witness. But it cannot be denied that the church is designed with earthly shepherds over the flock. And we are to respect them as such.

When we respect our leaders, their work becomes "a joy, not a burden" (v. 17). And if their work is a joy, it will be done with excellence. If leaders know they are not respected, they will not be able to work to full capacity. Their spirits will be too burdened.

A REQUEST (HEB. 13:18–19)

It is beautiful to read the author's humble request for prayer. The letter to the Hebrews is a masterpiece in every way. The rhetoric and logic are airtight. The theology is brilliant. The writing is inspiring. But here, the writer became one of us: a Christian in need of prayer.

He asked the readers to "pray for us" (v. 18). We don't know who he included, but Timothy is likely part of "us," because he is mentioned in verse 23. The writer and those with him knew they were justified by the blood of Christ, and they were trying to lead lives that honor God. They requested prayer for the wherewithal to do so. And the writer requested prayer that he would be with the recipients again. We don't know what had caused the separation. We don't even know the exact nature of his relationship to them. But it is moving to read about his longing to be with them. Everyone needs fellowship.

THE BENEDICTION (HEB. 13:20–21)

A word of benediction, a "good word," a "special blessing" is pronounced over the readers. For the first time, the writer mentioned the physical resurrection of Christ, here as the book winds down! He wrote that "the God of peace" brought Jesus back from the dead (v. 20). This was done through the power of the blood of the eternal covenant—the covenant we claim.

The writer requested that God would "equip you with everything good for doing his will" (v. 21). We know our consciences have been completely wiped clean. Our sin has been erased, and the power of sin has been canceled. Should we need anything else—any gift, any resource—may God provide it!

The writer requested that God help us to do all that pleases him through Christ. Because this is through the power of Jesus Christ, all glory goes to him. Because he made us perfect by his precious blood, all glory goes to him. Throughout all eternity, all glory goes to him.

Write a brief prayer in which you commit yourself to whatever work will please Christ. Praise and glorify him in your prayer.

FINAL GREETINGS (HEB. 13:22–25)

The author had pleaded at many points in this letter with the people he loved. He did so again as he urged them to give attention to what he had written—which he said was only a short letter. Brief though it may be, Hebrews may be the most profound epistle in the New Testament.

The last words are simple personal greetings and news. Timothy was apparently in prison, although we don't have information about that in any other books. Our writer hoped to join Timothy and make his way to see the Hebrews. Clearly, these were people he loved and missed. That love was shown in the way he had urged them to stay the course, to keep the faith.

Finally, the writer prayed that God's grace would rest on his readers. And he had gone a long way to make that happen. He had brought instruction and encouragement. He had carefully crafted this great epistle so that his readers might understand what a glorious, exalted High Priest they had, what a liberating covenant they had received, and what freedom they had to lead a life that would please God.

Hopefully, the recipients absorbed all of those wonderful lessons from this great epistle. And hopefully, so have we.

REFLECTION QUESTIONS

1. What is your attitude toward your pastor (or officer)? When speaking with others, do you engage in criticism of your spiritual leaders?

2. Confess any inappropriate feelings toward your spiritual leaders. Write a prayer for one of those leaders.

3. How has studying the book of Hebrews encouraged deeper worship in your life?

NOTES

PROLOGUE

1. Christology is defined by Merriam-Webster.com as "theological interpretation of the person and work of Christ."

2. Donald Guthrie, *Hebrews: An Introduction and Commentary*, Tyndale New Testament Commentaries, ed. Leon Morris, vol. 1 (Downers Grove, IL: InterVarsity Press, 1983).

INTRODUCTION

1. Donald Guthrie, *Hebrews: An Introduction and Commentary*, Tyndale New Testament Commentaries, ed. Leon Morris, vol. 1 (Downers Grove, IL: InterVarsity Press, 1983), 21.

2. Why "nearly always"? First Corinthians was not received with open arms, so in 2 Corinthians Paul had to be sure to establish his authority.

3. Gareth L. Cockerill, *Hebrews: A Commentary for Bible Students*, rev. ed. (Indianapolis: Wesleyan Publishing House, 2012), 13.

4. Peter T. O'Brien, *The Letter to the Hebrews* (Grand Rapids, MI: Eerdmans, 2010), 8.

5. Guthrie, *Hebrews*, 25.

6. *Tanakh* stands for Torah (the Law), *Nevi'im* stands for the Prophets, and *Ketuvim* stands for the Writings, such as Psalms and Proverbs.

7. F. F. Bruce, *The Epistle to the Hebrews*, rev. ed. (Grand Rapids, MI: Eerdmans, 1990), 6.

8. Cockerill, *Hebrews*, 17.

9. Although the text actually uses the word *tabernacle*, the word *tabernacle* may have been more synonymous with *temple* in the minds of the people of that day, whereas we tend to make a clear distinction.

DEVOTION 1

1. Donald Guthrie, *Hebrews: An Introduction and Commentary*, Tyndale New Testament Commentaries, ed. Leon Morris, vol. 1 (Downers Grove, IL: InterVarsity Press, 1983), 69.

2. Peter T. O'Brien, *The Letter to the Hebrews* (Grand Rapids, MI: Eerdmans, 2010), 51.

3. Guthrie, *Hebrews*, 69.

4. F. F. Bruce, *The Epistle to the Hebrews*, rev. ed. (Grand Rapids, MI: Eerdmans, 1990), 47.

5. For a brief but enlightening discussion on the notion of divine wisdom Christology, especially as it interfaces with high priestly Christology, see William Lane, *Word Biblical Commentary*, vol. 47a (Nashville: Thomas Nelson, 1991), 17–18.

DEVOTION 2

1. The word *shekinah* indicates the dwelling of God, making his presence among people. F. Brown, S. Driver, and C. Briggs, *The Brown-Driver-Briggs Hebrew and English Lexicon* (Peabody, MA: Hendrickson, 1994), 1016.

2. *The Salvation Army Handbook of Doctrine* (London: Salvation Books, 2010), 51.

3. Harold O. J. Brown, *Heresies: Heresy and Orthodoxy in the History of the Church* (Peabody, MA: Hendrickson, 1988), 97.

4. *The Salvation Army Handbook*, 25.

5. John MacArthur, *Hebrews: An Expository Commentary*, The MacArthur New Testament Commentary (Chicago: Moody, 1983), 19–20.

DEVOTION 3

1. William Lane, *Word Biblical Commentary*, vol. 47a (Nashville: Thomas Nelson, 1991), 25–26.

DEVOTION 4

1. Kevin L. Anderson, *Hebrews: A Commentary in the Wesleyan Tradition*, New Beacon Bible Commentary (Kansas City, MO: Beacon Hill, 2013), 77.

DEVOTION 5

1. William Lane, *Word Biblical Commentary*, vol. 47a (Nashville: Thomas Nelson, 1991), 46.

2. Gareth L. Cockerill, *Hebrews: A Commentary for Bible Students*, rev. ed. (Indianapolis: Wesleyan Publishing House, 2012), 60.

DEVOTION 6

1. Peter T. O'Brien, *The Letter to the Hebrews* (Grand Rapids, MI: Eerdmans, 2010), 103.

2. Ibid., 109.

DEVOTION 7

1. Peter T. O'Brien, *The Letter to the Hebrews* (Grand Rapids, MI: Eerdmans, 2010), 137.

DEVOTION 9

1. Kevin L. Anderson, *Hebrews: A Commentary in the Wesleyan Tradition*, New Beacon Bible Commentary (Kansas City, MO: Beacon Hill, 2013), 142.

2. Peter T. O'Brien, *The Letter to the Hebrews* (Grand Rapids, MI: Eerdmans, 2010), 159.

DEVOTION 10

1. The first two devotions in this book explored the divinity of Jesus and may be of service if the reader struggles with this.

2. Kevin L. Anderson, *Hebrews: A Commentary in the Wesleyan Tradition*, New Beacon Bible Commentary (Kansas City, MO: Beacon Hill, 2013), 169.

3. Ibid., 170.

DEVOTION 11

1. Gareth L. Cockerill, *Hebrews: A Commentary for Bible Students*, rev. ed. (Indianapolis: Wesleyan Publishing House, 2012), 134.

DEVOTION 12

1. Donald Guthrie, *Hebrews: An Introduction and Commentary*, Tyndale New Testament Commentaries, ed. Leon Morris, vol. 1 (Downers Grove, IL: InterVarsity Press, 1983), 148.

2. John MacArthur, *Hebrews: An Expository Commentary*, The MacArthur New Testament Commentary (Chicago: Moody, 1983), xiii.

3. Ibid., 144.

4. Gareth L. Cockerill, *Hebrews: A Commentary for Bible Students*, rev. ed. (Indianapolis: Wesleyan Publishing House, 2012), 138.

5. Peter T. O'Brien, *The Letter to the Hebrews* (Grand Rapids, MI: Eerdmans, 2010), 226.

DEVOTION 13

1. Gareth L. Cockerill, *Hebrews: A Commentary for Bible Students*, rev. ed. (Indianapolis: Wesleyan Publishing House, 2012), 144.

2. Kevin L. Anderson, *Hebrews: A Commentary in the Wesleyan Tradition*, New Beacon Bible Commentary (Kansas City, MO: Beacon Hill, 2013), 199.

3. Hebrews uses many legal terms. The writer of Hebrews was a brilliant rhetorician. The pursuit of rhetorical excellence in ancient times was mainly for application in courts of law. For more on legal terms in Hebrews, see Anderson, *Hebrews*, 197–198.

4. Cockerill, *Hebrews*, 145.

DEVOTION 14

1. William Lane, *Word Biblical Commentary*, vol. 47a (Nashville: Thomas Nelson, 1991), 164.

2. Kevin L. Anderson, *Hebrews: A Commentary in the Wesleyan Tradition*, New Beacon Bible Commentary (Kansas City, MO: Beacon Hill, 2013), 220.

3. Ibid., 221.

4. Gareth L. Cockerill, *Hebrews: A Commentary for Bible Students*, rev. ed. (Indianapolis: Wesleyan Publishing House, 2012), 159.

DEVOTION 15

1. Gareth L. Cockerill, *Hebrews: A Commentary for Bible Students*, rev. ed. (Indianapolis: Wesleyan Publishing House, 2012), 159.

2. F. F. Bruce, *The Epistle to the Hebrews*, rev. ed. (Grand Rapids, MI: Eerdmans, 1990), 172.

DEVOTION 16

1. Donald Guthrie, *Hebrews: An Introduction and Commentary*, Tyndale New Testament Commentaries, ed. Leon Morris, vol. 1 (Downers Grove, IL: InterVarsity Press, 1983), 173.

2. Kevin L. Anderson, *Hebrews: A Commentary in the Wesleyan Tradition*, New Beacon Bible Commentary (Kansas City, MO: Beacon Hill, 2013), 236.

3. F. F. Bruce, *The Epistle to the Hebrews*, rev. ed. (Grand Rapids, MI: Eerdmans, 1990), 190–191.

4. Peter T. O'Brien, *The Letter to the Hebrews* (Grand Rapids, MI: Eerdmans, 2010), 300.

5. Ibid., 302.

DEVOTION 17

1. William Lane, *Word Biblical Commentary*, vol. 47b (Nashville: Thomas Nelson, 2000), 220.

2. Kevin L. Anderson, *Hebrews: A Commentary in the Wesleyan Tradition*, New Beacon Bible Commentary (Kansas City, MO: Beacon Hill, 2013), 244.

3. F. F. Bruce, *The Epistle to the Hebrews*, rev. ed. (Grand Rapids, MI: Eerdmans, 1990), 208.

4. Ibid., 209.

DEVOTION 18

1. Peter T. O'Brien, *The Letter to the Hebrews* (Grand Rapids, MI: Eerdmans, 2010), 324.

2. William Lane, *Word Biblical Commentary*, vol. 47b (Nashville: Thomas Nelson, 2000), 225.

3. Ibid., 240.

DEVOTION 19

1. Donald Guthrie, *Hebrews: An Introduction and Commentary*, Tyndale New Testament Commentaries, ed. Leon Morris, vol. 1 (Downers Grove, IL: InterVarsity Press, 1983), 193.

2. Kevin L. Anderson, *Hebrews: A Commentary in the Wesleyan Tradition*, New Beacon Bible Commentary (Kansas City, MO: Beacon Hill, 2013), 250.

DEVOTION 20

1. F. F. Bruce, *The Epistle to the Hebrews*, rev. ed. (Grand Rapids, MI: Eerdmans, 1990), 228.

2. *The Salvation Army Handbook of Doctrine* (London: Salvation Books, 2010), 201.

3. Bruce, *Epistle*, 233.

DEVOTION 21

1. Gareth L. Cockerill, *Hebrews: A Commentary for Bible Students*, rev. ed. (Indianapolis: Wesleyan Publishing House, 2012), 197.

2. Ibid., 197–198.

3. William Lane, *Word Biblical Commentary*, vol. 47b (Nashville: Thomas Nelson, 2000), 261.

4. F. F. Bruce, *The Epistle to the Hebrews*, rev. ed. (Grand Rapids, MI: Eerdmans, 1990), 243.

DEVOTION 22

1. Kevin L. Anderson, *Hebrews: A Commentary in the Wesleyan Tradition*, New Beacon Bible Commentary (Kansas City, MO: Beacon Hill, 2013), 274.

2. Gareth L. Cockerill, *Hebrews: A Commentary for Bible Students*, rev. ed. (Indianapolis: Wesleyan Publishing House, 2012), 213.

3. William Lane, *Word Biblical Commentary*, vol. 47b (Nashville: Thomas Nelson, 2000), 287.

4. Donald Guthrie, *Hebrews: An Introduction and Commentary*, Tyndale New Testament Commentaries, ed. Leon Morris, vol. 1 (Downers Grove, IL: InterVarsity Press, 1983), 216.

5. John MacArthur, *Hebrews: An Expository Commentary*, The MacArthur New Testament Commentary (Chicago: Moody, 1983), 263.

DEVOTION 23

1. William Lane, *Word Biblical Commentary*, vol. 47b (Nashville: Thomas Nelson, 2000), 292.

2. Kevin L. Anderson, *Hebrews: A Commentary in the Wesleyan Tradition*, New Beacon Bible Commentary (Kansas City, MO: Beacon Hill, 2013), 280.

3. John MacArthur, *Hebrews: An Expository Commentary*, The MacArthur New Testament Commentary (Chicago: Moody, 1983), 270.

4. Peter T. O'Brien, *The Letter to the Hebrews* (Grand Rapids, MI: Eerdmans, 2010), 375.

5. Lane, *Word*, 292.

DEVOTION 25

1. William Lane, *Word Biblical Commentary*, vol. 47b (Nashville: Thomas Nelson, 2000), 340.

2. Gareth L. Cockerill, *Hebrews: A Commentary for Bible Students*, rev. ed. (Indianapolis: Wesleyan Publishing House, 2012), 243.

DEVOTION 26

1. Peter T. O'Brien, *The Letter to the Hebrews* (Grand Rapids, MI: Eerdmans, 2010), 423.

2. William Lane, *Word Biblical Commentary*, vol. 47b (Nashville: Thomas Nelson, 2000), 373.

DEVOTION 27

1. Gareth L. Cockerill, *Hebrews: A Commentary for Bible Students*, rev. ed. (Indianapolis: Wesleyan Publishing House, 2012), 265.

DEVOTION 28

1. Gareth L. Cockerill, *Hebrews: A Commentary for Bible Students*, rev. ed. (Indianapolis: Wesleyan Publishing House, 2012), 274.

2. These thoughts were taken from Kevin Anderson, *Hebrews: A Commentary in the Wesleyan Tradition*, New Beacon Bible Commentary (Kansas City, MO: Beacon Hill, 2013), 322.

3. William Lane, *Word Biblical Commentary*, vol. 47b (Nashville: Thomas Nelson, 2000), 428.

4. "Runner Helps Rival Runner at State," YouTube video, posted by Benjamin Rife, June 6, 2012, https://www.youtube.com/watch?v=IiQ4SNkx_Z8.

DEVOTION 29

1. Things that are "eschatological" have to do with the end of the world and/or human history—what will occur when Jesus returns.

2. F. F. Bruce, *The Epistle to the Hebrews*, rev. ed. (Grand Rapids, MI: Eerdmans, 1990), 356.

DEVOTION 31

1. Gareth L. Cockerill, *Hebrews: A Commentary for Bible Students*, rev. ed. (Indianapolis: Wesleyan Publishing House, 2012), 306.